DAVID WILLIAMSON was bo[rn...]
brought up in Bairnsdale, nor[...]
graduate in Mechanical Enginee[ring...]
and was a lecturer in thermo-dy[namics ... psychology]
at Swinburn Institute of Technology until 1973. His first full-length play, *The Coming of Stork*, had its premiere at the La Mama Theatre, Carlton in 1970 and later became the film *Stork*, directed by Tim Burstall.

The Removalists and *Don's Party*, both written in 1971, were quickly taken up and performed around Australia, then in London and later made into films with screenplays by the author. In 1972 *The Removalists* won the Australian Writers' Guild Awgie Award for the best stage play and the best script in any medium. In 1973 David Williamson was nominated the most promising playwright by the London *Evening Standard* following the British production of *The Removalists*.

The next play was *Jugglers Three* (1972) commissioned by the Melbourne Theatre Company; followed by *What If You Died Tomorrow* (1973) for the Old Tote Theatre Company; *The Department* (1975) and *A Handful of Friends* (1976) for the South Australian Theatre Company. *The Club* (1977) broke all previous box office records and in 1978 had seasons at the Kennedy Centre, Washington, on Broadway and in Berlin. In 1980 the Nimrod Theatre production went to London. The film, directed by Bruce Beresford, was released in 1980. *Travelling North* was performed around Australia in 1979 and in London in 1980. The film version was released in 1987. It was followed by *Celluloid Heroes* (1980), *The Perfectionist* (1982), *Sons of Cain* (1985) and *Emerald City* (1987) which played in London and New York in 1988. The film version of *Emerald City* was released in 1989. *Top Silk* was first produced in Sydney and Melbourne in the same year, followed by *Siren* in 1990. *Money and Friends* was performed around Australia in 1991, in Los Angeles in 1992 and in London in 1993. *Brilliant Lies* was first produced in Brisbane in 1993.

David Williamson has won the Australian Film Institute film script award for *Petersen* (1974), *Don's Party* (1976),

Gallipoli (1981) and *Travelling North* (1987) and has won eleven Australian Writers' Guild Awgie Awards. He lives in Sydney with his novelist wife Kristin Williamson. Between them they have five children.

Also by David Williamson:
The Removalists
Don's Party
The Department
A Handful of Friends
The Club
Travelling North
The Perfectionist
Sons of Cain
Collected Plays Volume I:
    The Coming of Stork
    Don's Party
    The Removalists
    Jugglers Three
    What if You Died Tomorrow
Emerald City
Top Silk
Siren
Money and Friends

Brilliant Lies

DAVID WILLIAMSON

CURRENCY PRESS • SYDNEY

CURRENCY PLAYS
General Editor: Katharine Brisbane

First published in 1993 by Currency Press Ltd
PO Box 452, Paddington NSW 2021, Australia
Copyright © David Williamson, 1993 *Brilliant Lies*,
© Aubrey Mellor 1993 *Perceptions of the truth*, © Greg Tillett 1993 *An inevitable part of life*

10 9 8 7 6 5 4 3

This book is copyright. Apart from any fair dealing for the purpose of private study, research or review, as permitted under the Copyright Act, no part may be reproduced by any process without written permission. Inquiries concerning publication, translation or recording rights should be addressed to the publishers.

Any performance or public reading of *Brilliant Lies* is forbidden unless a licence has been received from the author or the author's agent. The purchase of this book in no way gives the purchaser the right to perform the play in public, whether by means of a staged production or a reading. All applications for public performance should be addressed to the author, c/- Anthony Williams Management, 50 Oxford St, Paddington NSW 2021

National Library of Australia
Cataloguing-in-Publication data
    Williamson, David, 1942-
        Brilliant lies.
    ISBN 0 86819 371 2.
    I. Title.
    A822.3

Printed by Southwood Press, Marrickville NSW
Cover design by Trevor Hood

To my wife Kristin for her continuing love,
editorial advice and support.

Lies Lies Lies Lies Lies Lies Lies Lies Lies

Contents

Acknowledgements · viii

Perceptions of the truth
Aubrey Mellor · ix

An inevitable part of life
Dr Greg Tillett · xi

BRILLIANT LIES

ACT ONE · 1

ACT TWO · 40

Acknowledgements

I'd like to thank my wife Kristin, my daughter Rebecca, Aubrey Mellor, Ray Barrett, Miranda Otto, Genevieve Lemon, Chris Betts, Christine Amor, Peter Adams, Rhett Walton and dramaturg and assistant director David Berthold for their feelings and opinions during the development of this play. I finally had to decide for myself what went on the page but their input undoubtedly gave me richer options.

D. W.

Photo Acknowledgements: Cover photo shows Miranda Otto as Susy, Christine Amor as Marion and Chris Betts as Gary in the Royal Queensland Theatre Company production of *Brilliant Lies*, presented by the Melbourne Theatre Company. Photographer: Jeff Busby. Back cover photo shows Ray Barrett as Brian and Miranda Otto as Susy in the same production. Photographer: Jeff Busby. p.vi Miranda Otto as Susy, Genevieve Lemon as Katy, Christine Amor as Marion, Peter Adams as Vince and Chris Betts as Gary in the RQTC production. Photographer: William Long. p.xx Miranda Otto as Susy in the RQTC production. Photographer: William Long. p.13 Genevieve Lemon as Katy and Rhett Walton as Paul in the RQTC production presented by the MTC. Photographer: Jeff Busby. p.27 Ray Barrett as Brian, Miranda Otto as Susy and Rhett Walton as Paul in the RQTC production. Photographer: William Long. p.55 Peter Adams as Vince and Chris Betts as Gary in the RQTC production. Photographer: William Long. p.63
Miranda Otto as Susy, Genevieve Lemon as Katy and Chris Betts as Gary in the RQTC production. Photographer: William Long.

Perceptions of the truth

Aubrey Mellor

'Much of the sadness, humour and drama of human life arises out of the inescapable differences between individuals.'
David Williamson

This black comedy started life as a drama. From its initial drafts the most powerful scenes were those which showed the clash between different perceptions of the truth - a male and female view of the same incident. The basis of *Brilliant Lies* is the current male backlash against feminism, informing all discussion of the play, its characters and its subject - sexual harassment at work.

As there is now a mechanism where overt sexism can be called to account, there is a fear amongst some men that women will abuse this process. Interestingly, the media and the Anti-discrimination Board alike presupposed that the play was going to expose the woman as liar. David Williamson has never been one to pull punches but he has taken pains to maintain the integrity of the Board. The play is as much about men trying to cope with the new social order as it is about women trying to alter the attitudes of men.

'I think the bulk of my work has been exploring or satirising the war between the sexes and this is a logical thing to be looking at ...I think there is a lot of heat in this area at the moment.' As in all his plays, Williamson's intention is to generate discussion of an important social concern by dramatising its salient points. 'Storyteller to the tribe doesn't mean that you keep telling bland stories...they can have a moral point, they can be endeavouring to change the tribe's perception in some way.' No sooner had his theme been made public than a flood of harassment cases dominated the Australian media, and interestingly too, in America David Mamet began to work on a similar theme for his play *Oleanna*.

I continue to be amazed by the bravery of Williamson's drafts of his plays. In pursuit of a thorough exploration of his themes, he takes giant leaps where others may merely tinker with a sentence. Yet through any number of drafts the commitment to the central theme does not waver. The most exciting leap in the development of this work was the decision to reflect harassment in the workplace with harassment in the home. In balancing this, care was taken to remain in the area of harassment, not assault or incest, but an area more difficult to define; the grey area where perception is tantamount to truth until a more enlightened view is accepted.

The title of the play comes from Williamson's own statement: 'To survive in the '90s you've either got to be lucky, rich, or able to tell brilliant lies'. Vince's old world propriety is less successful than Gary's brash scheming and in presenting those who are not 'brilliant liars' as failures, Williamson is calling into question the moral structure of our society. Yet this is the first play in recent times where he has focussed on a younger generation of protagonists and moved away from the familiar Williamson world of the middle-aged and middle-class, to a world of twenty and thirty-year-olds struggling to find their own place in Australian society.

And what of the 'truth'? Those who are shocked by Susy's revelation of the lie of the fifty dollar note, should consider the alternative: that in a locked room, under threat, she had no choice but comply with Gary's demand. In Susy's case the lie makes the truth easier to tell.

Brisbane, 1993

An inevitable part of life

Dr Greg Tillett

Conflict is an inevitable and pervasive part of life. Sometimes it is resolved creatively, promoting better communication, stronger relationships and a richer experience of life. Often it is not resolved, but results either in lingering distress and continually painful relationships or in violent (usually emotional but sometimes physical) eruptions, the ending of a relationship and long-term bitterness. The more intense the relationship in which the conflict occurs and the more personally challenging (or threatening) the issues on which it focuses, the more likely it is to result in fighting, or avoidance or displacement. Thus life may become, in the words of one of the characters in *Brilliant Lies*, 'this appalling, bruising, humiliating state of interpersonal warfare'.

David Williamson's *Brilliant Lies* is certain to provoke controversy. He raises the complex, complicated and often confusing issues which surround allegations of sexual harassment. Such harassment is often assumed to consist simply of an allegation which is either demonstrably true or demonstrably false. As with most things in life, it is rarely that simple. Workplace interactions are no different to interactions outside the workplace. Men and women at work, brought together, not necessarily by choice, find themselves in close proximity for a substantial proportion of their time. It is, of course, a myth that the private person is left at home when the work person goes to the office. Private and professional dimensions blend and blur, and not necessarily harmoniously.

Interpersonal and family conflicts intrude into the workplace, just as workplace conflicts are carried over into private life. Those involved in each sphere become participants, indirectly and often invisibly, in conflicts in the other. Thus in *Brilliant Lies* Susy's family are players in her employment conflict with Gary and Vince, and the conflict originating in her former workplace intrudes into her relationships with her father, her sister and her brother. Likewise, although the text provides less evidence of it, one assumes that Gary's conflicts at home and at work are inextricably linked.

This play also focuses on the question: what is truth? There is a popular assumption that people either tell the truth or they lie, but in describing events in their experience, human beings rarely do either in absolute terms. There are frequently shades of truth, statements which are partly true and partly not, or true as far as the individual making them understands, but not (if the term has any real meaning) objectively true. Individuals often seek to strengthen the truth of what they say by adding enhancing details, or diminishing elements of what others are saying. This is not necessarily dishonest. It is often an unconscious process intended to achieve an outcome which the individual considers fair or just. Is Susy's use of her sister, Katy, a legitimate attempt to strengthen a case based on real harassment, but somewhat lacking in substance, or a conspiracy to trap Gary and Vince into parting with money? As Gary describes it: 'this bullshit story to screw money out of us'.

Brilliant Lies also addresses the quest for justice. It is often overlooked that a desire for justice is one of the most powerful motivators in human conduct, particularly in cases of conflict. Many women who allege sexual harassment in the workplace want nothing more (or less) than justice, and fight to achieve that even when the very fight seems to substantially diminish their chances of obtaining it. They often seek an acknowledgement that their claim was true, that they were treated unfairly and inappropriately. There is within most people, it seems, a stong desire that the world be coherently fair, that good triumph, that virtue be rewarded and wickedness be punished. As naive as that hope may be, it is a strong drive, pushing those in conflict to seek to achieve the vindication of the innocent and the punishment of the guilty, almost at any price.

Those reading or seeing this play will face a number of dilemmas, all of which are faced regularly by those who investigate and seek to resolve allegations of sexual harassment. Is Susy telling the truth? Is it the whole, unvarnished and unenhanced truth? Or is she telling some truth, around which she is weaving a supporting fabrication to strengthen her chances of receiving what she considers to be justice? As Susy herself says: 'It didn't happen *exactly* as I told it, so what!' This, of course, raises difficult moral and legal questions.

If some of what Susy says is true, and some of what she says is false, what entitlement ought she to have to compensation for that which is true? Should compensation be diminished by her apparent exaggeration? Should Gary be compensated for any elements of falsehood in her allegations against him?

And there is a dilemma for those accused of sexual harassment and their employers, as Gary and Vince readily recognise. Gary declares: 'I'm in a no win situation. If this goes to court I'm going to lose out even if I win. There'll be jokes behind my back for the rest of my life and my wife and kids will suffer. If I want to preserve my reputation I've got to pay money.' An allegation of sexual harassment alone certainly can damage reputation: many people believe that smoke only occurs if there is fire, and that if an action is not successful it may be more because of legal technicalities than because of the innocence of the person accused.

This has led some critics of the law on sexual harassment to suggest that it constitutes an open opportunity for blackmail. Might a person accused, or an employer (who is generally legally liable in such matters), pay simply to avoid publicity, regardless of the truth of the allegation? The reality is almost certainly that they do not. As with all allegations of sexual misconduct, the burden of proof is on the person making the allegation, and the process of a judicial hearing is incredibly stressful. Even knowing the allegation to be true, few women would willingly pursue an allegation through the threatening maze of legal process if they believed that the result would be against them. In addition, it is likely that the person complaining will suffer severe damage to her reputation and future employment prospects as her claim and almost inevitably her character, is subject to public examination.

Sexual harassment rarely occurs in the presence of independent witnesses, or indeed, of any witnesses. Allegations are therefore usually the word of one person against another. How is the truth to be ascertained? In most jurisdictions dealing with sexual harassment, judicial bodies seek to determine such matters by testing the credibility of claim and counter-claim 'on the balance of probabilities'. This assumes that the matter remains in the civil arena. If a crime has been committed (as it may have been if Gary assaulted Susy by taking hold of her breasts), and it moves into the criminal courts, the allegations must be tested and proved 'beyond reasonable doubt'. Where the word of one person is contrasted with the word of another, it is unclear how there could be no element of reasonable doubt.

Employers are likely to face almost insurmountable difficulties in deciding who is telling the truth. Traditionally, they have tended to assume that the male employee is of greater value to the organisation, that the woman is a trouble-maker, and her employment is terminated. Of course, most women do not allow matters to go that far. They endure harassment until they can endure it no more, and then they resign.

Although workplaces are improving in their approaches to complaints of sexual harassment, there is still a tendency to disbelieve allegations, especially where they are made against someone who is assumed to be a 'good bloke'. When Susy complains to her boss, Vince, and Gary denies her allegation, Vince, not atypically, simply assumes she is lying and dismisses her as a result. It is not uncommon for employers to take such a view of sexual harassment complainants. If the employer accepts that something happened, in sexual harassment (as in rape) it is not uncommon for them to attribute it to the behaviour or the appearance of the woman, who was obviously 'asking for it'. Thus, Gary and Vince seek to get in a pre-emptive strike against Susy by telling Marion that Susy dressed with 'everything showing'. Even her brother, Paul, is shocked by the allegation of sexual harassment because he believes Susy to be a promiscuous 'tart' who 'dresses like a tart'.

The personal, and particularly the sexual, reputation of women making complaints of sexual harassment may be raised for scrutiny, either in workplace investigations (and certainly in workplace gossip) or in judicial proceedings. The parallels with allegations of rape are obvious. Is Susy honest? Does she have a reputation for lying and if she does, how can anything she now says be believed? Even Susy's brother, Paul, remains unconvinced of her allegations, recalling that she has always told 'brilliant lies'.

The possibility of doubt, and the suggestion that some women may either fabricate claims of sexual harassment, or at least exaggerate such claims, is inherent in David Williamson's work. It is therefore likely to be highly controversial. There are those who would declare that, in a patriarchal society, women are inevitably going to be the victims of male violence (whether in physical abuse or in the exercise of other forms of power), and that all claims of sexual harassment are true. Conversely, there are those who will argue that there is something of a sexual harassment 'industry', actively promoted by radical feminists, with women rushing to make allegations in the hope of gaining some benefit, like monetary compensation, or with the aim of injuring men.

Clearly, neither claim is true. In the experience of dealing with complaints of sexual harassment under legislation like the New South Wales Anti-Discrimination Act and the federal Sex Discrimination Act, agencies across Australia report that it is extremely rare to find an allegation where there was not some clear evidence that *something* had happened. The nature of what had happened, its appropriateness and acceptability, and the extent to which it could be considered normal workplace behaviour, or, more frequently, normal male behaviour, are usually the critical issues.

The range of what was seen to constitute normal male behaviour in the workplace covers a broad, and surprising, range. In some cases, what is clearly criminal assault may be regarded, at least by the employer, as 'what blokes do'.

Women in the workplace may accept such a view. Indeed, cases are seen in which women in a workplace have simply accepted over a long period behaviour which, on the face of it, constituted sexual harassment, and are not necessarily supportive of new female staff who take offence at it. But changing times, increasing awareness amongst women of their rights, and the occasional publicity surrounding a case of sexual harassment and resulting nervousness on the part of some employers, has changed the levels of tolerance in at least the more overt forms of sexual harassment.

Rules about behaviour between men and women, including sexual behaviour, have undergone something of a revolution in the last few decades. But the revolution has not finished, and that's where some of the problems arise. Just what constitutes appropriate behaviour by a man to a woman in the workplace is not readily definable in specific terms. Presumably assault, including grabbing hold of the breasts, or direct demands for sex, or indecent exposure are all unacceptable. Problems most often arise with what is sometimes called humorous banter, or flattering remarks, expressions of interest and indications of attraction. Where is the line to be drawn? And by whom? And how can such restrictions on what some men may regard as normal behaviour be enforced without creating such tension, discomfort and hostility in the workplace as to make it intolerable?

Certainly, some men seem to be having severe difficulty in adapting to what they view as the new rules, where behaviour which may have been tolerated by women in the past is now likely to be the subject of complaint. As Susy's sister Katy comments: 'After thousands of years of abuse, males are finally being held accountable, and you don't like it.' This may be the feminist perspective. It is certainly not typical of a male response, which is likely to attribute supposed changes of what is acceptable to a militant minority of radical feminists with a vicious hatred of men.

How should sexual attraction in the workplace be dealt with? It would be naive to imagine that it can be left outside or even successfully repressed. Do men and women have radically different approaches to sexual attraction and if so, does this have implications in the workplace? Certainly, many men seem to believe it does, and might well echo the comment by Susy's father: 'One day you bloody feminists are going to realise that men *aren't* like women. We have a sex drive that's demanding and insistent!'

For many men the answer seems simple enough: if a woman should find the attentions of a man undesirable, (for reasons which will always be totally incomprehensible to the man concerned) she should simply tell him so. Presumably he, being reasonable, will then stop. Many women feel a sense of personal inadequacy in responding to sexual harassment. As Susy says: 'I just thought Gary was pathetic, and that I should be able to cope with it myself.'

The reality, however, is that those who engage in sexual harassment are exercising their power rather than their sexuality, and for that very reason their victims are unlikely to feel sufficiently powerful to object. If she needs the job, or fears repercussions, the woman may have excellent reasons for enduring without overt objection. And there is no evidence that those who sexually harass, unlike those who are simply expressing a genuine attraction, are reasonable men who desist when asked to do so.

What, then, does the woman do? She may endure the situation, suffer increasing stress, probably take more sick leave, and generally become a less than satisfactory employee, for whom resignation or termination is the inevitable outcome. Or she can complain. But without substantiation of the allegation, and particularly in the face of a less than sympathetic employer, this option may make things far worse rather than better. Or she can go to an external agency, such as the New South Wales Anti-Discrimination Board or the federal Sex Discrimination Commissioner.

Brilliant Lies raises a question of the role of the mediator or conciliator from a body like the Anti-Discrimination Board. In the play, the Board is represented by a mediator, Marion. She is hardly a model of professional competence, more because of her outspoken remarks about her own agenda than anything else.

Theoretically neutral, such conciliators are expected by law to investigate and to attempt to resolve by conciliation complaints that come to them. Obviously conciliators do reach conclusions about the probability of a complaint being true. The legislation under which they work includes provision for complaints to be declined which are deemed to be frivolous, vexatious, misconceived or lacking in substance. Conciliators are caught in several binds. On the one hand they are expected to be neutral and on the other to make some conclusion about the probability of the allegations being true.

Most have a strong sense of social justice and a commitment to the defence of the oppressed.

Can this lead to conciliators becoming advocates for the person making the complaint and in effect, prosecutors of the person against whom the complaint is made? Certainly Gary and Vince believe this is the case, and Marion, in a conversation with Katy also suggests that it is: 'I get a lot of harassment cases in here and in almost every case I'm totally convinced that the woman involved has been put through a vicious and degrading humiliation. I try and stay neutral, but the truth is I'm usually on their side, and I think I should be.' Just how conciliators are supposed to deal with personal values and prejudice, while remaining neutral, is yet to be adequately explained.

Brilliant Lies is a work which is sure to provoke discussion and controversy. It raises many difficult and challenging issues which may appear to have been enhanced for a dramatic performance, yet the play confronts situations which are very close to reality. The characters struggle less to analyse and resolve their situation than to displace and suppress it. In so doing, they merely initiate new conflicts and reinforce old, inadequate patterns of dealing with them. The reader would do well to contemplate what (if anything) might have been a more creative approach.

Dr Greg Tillett is Director of The Centre for Conflict Resolution at Macquarie University in Sydney. He was previously Senior Conciliation Officer with the New South Wales Anti-Discrimination Board.

Lies Lies Lies Lies Lies Lies Lies Lies Lies Lies Lies

Brilliant Lies was first performed by the Royal Queensland Theatre Company on 29 April 1993 at the Suncorp Theatre, Brisbane with the following cast:

MARION	Christine Amor
SUSY	Miranda Otto
VINCE	Peter Adams
GARY	Chris Betts
KATY	Genevieve Lemon
BRIAN	Ray Barrett
PAUL	Rhett Walton

Director, Aubrey Mellor
Designer, Dale Ferguson
Lighting Designer, David Walters

CHARACTERS

MARION, official mediator from the anti-discrimination commission.
SUSY, a young, ambitious career woman
VINCE, owner of the company where Susy works
GARY, Susy's manager
KATY, Susy's sister
BRIAN, Susy's father
PAUL, Susy's brother

SETTING

The play is set in the offices of LifeChoice Options, an office gymnasium, Susy and Katy's home and Brian's home.

Act One

A conference room. Functional but soothing. MARION LEE, *an attractive woman in her mid-to-late thirties sits facing* SUSY CONNOR. SUSY *is in her mid-twenties, very attractive, very vivacious, very personable.*

MARION: Can you give me examples?
SUSY: Of the harassment? Sure. It went on continually from the moment I arrived, but if you want the highlight, it was the time I was asked to stay back late just before I was fired.
MARION: What happened?
SUSY: What happened. When we were the only two left in the building he turned to me and said, 'This is boring. Let's talk sex'. Gary's not subtle.
MARION: What did you say?
SUSY: I said, 'Gary, you have been talking sex to me for the last seven months. I don't find it titillating, and I don't find it amusing, so please stop'. Then he said, 'Do you want to keep your job here?' I said, 'Yes'. No prizes for guessing what happened next.
MARION: [*with her notebook poised*] Unfortunately I do need to know what happened next – with as much precise detail as you can remember.
SUSY: [*frowning, concentrating*] I was sitting at the computer. He came up behind me. I concentrated as hard as I could on the screen, then suddenly there were two hands on my breasts and he said something sick making like, 'The twin peaks of womanhood. Soft, sweet, seductive'. I froze and when I turned around Gary's member was inches in front of my nose. I ran.
    [MARION *scribbles furiously on her notepad, then looks up at* SUSY.]

I went to Vince – Vince owns the business – next morning and told him what had happened. He called Gary into the office and asked if it was true. Gary denied everything. Vince sent me out. I heard them arguing. Vince called me back in and fired me.
    [MARION *looks at her.*]
MARION: You heard Vince and Gary arguing?
SUSY: I'm sure Vince must know what a sleaze Gary is, but he depends so heavily on Gary that he had no choice.
MARION: Before this incident Gary talked sex over the inter-office phone?
SUSY: [*nodding*] Gary had an office that overlooked my wordprocessor. I'd pick up the phone and Gary would start to tell me some vile fantasy.
MARION: What kind of fantasy?
SUSY: Which position he was screwing me from, how he was doing it – I was usually so shocked he got two or three seconds in before I hung up. And the fantasies got progressively worse.
MARION: Why didn't you go to – [*Consulting her pad.*] Vince, earlier.
SUSY: I just thought Gary was pathetic, and that I should be able to cope with it myself.
MARION: You didn't talk about it to any of the other women there?
SUSY: There were only four and they weren't exactly friendly.
MARION: Why not?
SUSY: Who knows.
    [*Pause*]
Because they . . .
MARION: Because they what?
SUSY: This is going to sound snobbish but they were – they resented the fact I wear decent clothes, that I didn't talk – [*Imitating a broad Australian accent*] like I just drove in from Rooty Hill, that I know most of the movers and

shakers of this city, that I had a decent education – those sort of things.
MARION: Decent education?
SUSY: I went to a good private school – and they didn't. Not that that makes any difference to me, but it obviously did to them.
MARION: Did you go to University?
SUSY: I went for a term, but I couldn't stand it. I went to Europe and lived in France and Italy for two years, then Dad went broke and that was that.
MARION: You came back and got this job?
SUSY: I came back and couldn't get a job. For nearly three years.
MARION: You know most of the movers and shakers of the city?
SUSY: It's one thing to meet them at nightclubs. It's another to get them to give you a job. I finally got mad at this guy who'd been sort of promising me a job in his ad agency for months, and he took me aside and said I had to understand that the market is flooded with girls like me with looks and personality, but that if I didn't get some real workplace skills I was no use to anyone.
MARION: Who supported you for those three years?
SUSY: Men. I fooled myself that I was having a series of deep and meaningfuls. The truth was I was passed from hand to hand around the half dozen or so wealthy unmarried heterosexual men left in this city. Three years on I found myself back where I started and realised that workskills were urgently needed.
MARION: Did you? Get some skills?
SUSY: I did a wordprocessing course. And finally after dozens of interviews I got a job.
MARION: Not the sort of job you were hoping to get?
SUSY: No. A firm of borderline shonky insurance brokers called LifeChoice Options was definitely not where I wanted to position myself in life.

MARION: Pretty bad, huh?
SUSY: [*nodding*] Charming little scams like recommending policies and not bothering to tell the client that the true rate of return they'd get at the end of their twenty years was not much better than burying their money in a tin at the bottom of their garden.
MARION: Your letter said you were an Assistant Manager.
SUSY: I assisted the manager.
MARION: Gary?
SUSY: Yeah. Vince is the owner, but Gary effectively runs the place.
MARION: Tell me a bit more about Gary.
SUSY: He did accountancy at some minor college, drives a Mazda MX5, married above himself, obviously doesn't get enough sex, has about as much style and panache as a particularly gauche gorilla, but thinks he's Mel Gibson with a dash of Kerry Packer.
   [MARION *laughs.*]
So? Where do I stand?
MARION: It seems a clear cut case of wrongful harassment and dismissal. If it goes to court the difficulty is going to be to prove it.
SUSY: It's basically my word against theirs?
MARION: Yes.
SUSY: I told my sister Katy about it. Right from the start. We rent a place together.
MARION: She'd be prepared to back you up?
SUSY: [*nodding*] She saw how upset it was making me. You said 'if' it goes to court?
MARION: The other side usually wants to solve this kind of dispute before it gets that far.
   [SUSY *looks at her*]
SUSY: Bad publicity?
MARION: [*nodding*] If it goes public the press are certain to pick it up and Gary and – [*Consulting her pad*] LifeChoice

ACT ONE 5

Options will get the sort of publicity I'm sure they don't want.

SUSY: [*nodding*] Gary would hate it. His wife's a North Shore princess. If Gary hits the headlines as Mr Gary *Twin Peaks* Fitzgerald, her family will order her to divorce.

MARION: How distressed did the harassment make you?

SUSY: I got incredibly distressed. If I'm blasé now it's a defence.

MARION: In part the compensation depends on the distress.

SUSY: I was very distressed.

[*Pause*]

I read some woman got forty thousand the other day.

MARION: That was very severe harassment and she had proof.

SUSY: Mine was severe. Very severe. And I have my sister to back me up.

* * *

Two men sit opposite MARION; VINCE WILLIAMS, *in his late fifties, wearing a very conventional suit, with ultra-neat hair and the accent and style of old suburban Australia and* GARY FITZGERALD, *in his thirties, tough and athletic, wearing an expensive but ill-fitting suit and with an air of ruthless cold competence.*

VINCE: By what right? On whose authority? A phone call out of the blue and we're summonsed in here like bad schoolboys.

MARION: The government has seen fit to pass laws –

VINCE: [*looking at* GARY] We know about those laws.

GARY: The 'make life hell for successful white male laws'.

MARION: Susy Connor has lodged a complaint with us that she was sexually harassed and then unfairly dismissed. I want to arrange a conciliation conference to try and settle this without having to go to court.

VINCE: We dismissed her because we found her work unsatisfactory.
MARION: Susy claims she was sexually harassed.
GARY: She wasn't.
VINCE: She told you that Gary had exposed himself and all that nonsense?
MARION: She told me that Gary had fondled her breasts, exposed himself and invited her to perform fellatio, yes, and that this was the culmination of seven months of severe phone harassment.
GARY: Absolute rubbish. Absolute nonsense.
VINCE: You want to know the truth about that girl. She came in with [*Searching for words*] – everything showing –
GARY: Boobs popping right out of her dress.
VINCE: Dress right up to here. [*Demonstrating a point right up his thigh.*] Blatant.
GARY: Trying to get herself the job.
MARION: She did get the job.
   [*The men look at each other, embarrassed.*]
VINCE: I wouldn't have given it to her.
MARION: Gary convinced you?
GARY: I thought she had potential.
   [MARION *looks at* GARY.]
MARION: Potential.
GARY: Work potential.
MARION: Right. [*With gentle irony*] So let's get this straight. An attractive young woman comes for a job interview in what you two seem to feel is a near naked state, but despite being shocked, even outraged, and despite the fact she has never held down a job before, you are both prepared to 'give her a go'. On the basis of her perceived work potential.
GARY: It's easy to see where your sympathies lie.
MARION: I'm trying to establish the facts. What was it about her that led you to think she might have work potential?
GARY: She seemed to have energy and drive.

MARION: Seemed?
VINCE: She had energy and drive all right. None of it exhibited during working hours.
GARY: She spent all her time on the phone organising her social life! No one could get through!
VINCE: We warned her time and time again. And every morning she'd come to work looking like –
GARY: Looking like she came straight to work from an all night drug party.
VINCE: She *told* one of the women she took drugs.
GARY: Ecstasy. She went to an ecstasy party.
VINCE: And had sex. She told a married woman. Who was shocked.
MARION: [*straight-faced*] Yes, as a married woman, sex and ecstasy *do* seem a startling combination.
VINCE: She used to go to sleep at her desk.
GARY: To recuperate before next night's party.
MARION: This sort of behaviour happened straight away?
GARY: The day after she was hired.
MARION: And you kept her on for seven months?
GARY: We kept hoping she'd . . . she had potential.
MARION: Of course. The potential. [*Gentle irony returns*] I'm still finding it hard to understand how a girl whose only activity while she was employed by you was to either sleep at her desk or phone her friends lasted seven months. If I was an employer I'd have her out of there in seven days. You're obviously an extremely *tolerant* employer Mr Williams.
VINCE: We've painted her a little bit worse than she was. Some times she was fun. Sometimes she could make you laugh. And she could knock out a decent letter when she felt like it. Gary was right. She did have potential.
GARY: Basically she thought she was too good for us.
MARION: Too good for you.
GARY: She wanted to be working in something more trendy than insurance.

MARION: I phoned the girl who Susy replaced. Rhonda Gibbs. Gary, Rhonda told me that you did make frequent sexual innuendoes in front of her and it was one of the reasons she left the job.
GARY: You've got no right to do that!
MARION: I'm trying to gather all the relevant information.
GARY: You can't bring up past behaviour in court.
MARION: This is an informal conciliation process. It's not a court.
GARY: Jesus, you can't tell a joke these days without getting told you're a sex fiend!
VINCE: [*nodding*] It's ridiculous. Is it compulsory? This conference? It's just her word against ours.
MARION: If you choose to you can refuse conciliation and the case will go straight to a legally binding public court. I would have thought there were reasons you wouldn't want it to go that far.
GARY: This is the sting, huh? We don't pay up I get my name in the papers?
MARION: The press tend to find these sort of cases newsworthy.
GARY: Yeah. Great choice, huh? Brave new world. Damned if you do, damned if you don't! Who needs proof any more when lies will get you the same results!
MARION: You want to try conciliation?
GARY: What choice have we got?
MARION: I'll try and make the process fair to both sides.
GARY: At the Anti-Discrimination Board? The very *name* indicates what side of the fence you're on right from the start.
MARION: I'm on the side of the truth.

* * *

ACT ONE

The tiny apartment SUSY *shares with her sister* KATY. KATY *is not as conventionally attractive as her sister, but her face is expressive and appealing. She is some years older than* SUSY. *Their older brother* PAUL, *whose body language is awkward and uneasy, tries to catch their attention as* SUSY *polishes her shoes and* KATY *works on a drawing.*

PAUL: Look, I made –
KATY: Susy! How many times have I told you not to do that on the carpet!
PAUL: Look, I made a real effort to come here tonight and I wonder if you could just listen to me for a second!
   [*The two sisters exchange glances. It is obvious they find their brother hard to take seriously. They tend to treat him with affectionate disdain.*]
   Dad is very upset.
SUSY: Why?
PAUL: Because you never call him, and when he calls you never tell him anything and if it's Susy – ten seconds in she gets another call and puts him on hold. Then never gets back.
SUSY: I forgot to get back once.
PAUL: Have you told him you've been fired?
SUSY: No.
PAUL: Don't you think he should know?
SUSY: I'll tell him when I'm ready.
PAUL: We had a long talk the other night and he is really, really sad that he isn't closer to you two. And he's really worried.
KATY: About what?
PAUL: About you losing your job. Heaven only knows what he'll think when he finds out about Susy.
KATY: I've got a job.
PAUL: Oh yeah. A qualified architect driving a taxi. Great.
KATY: Half the architects in the city are out of work. What

the hell does he expect? He hasn't been a shining success himself lately.
PAUL: How do you think he feels about that?
SUSY: We've all got problems.
PAUL: What are your plans, Susy?
SUSY: I'm fine.
PAUL: Sure.
SUSY: I'm fine. I'm taking them to court and they're going to have to pay a lot of money.
PAUL: Unfair dismissal? You'll get a couple of thousand at the most.
SUSY: Unfair dismissal plus sexual harassment.
PAUL: Sexual harassment?
SUSY: Yes. What's so strange about that?
PAUL: For someone as . . .
SUSY: Someone as what?
PAUL: [*hesitating*] You're not exactly chaste.
  [KATY *and* SUSY *voice a chorus of protest.*]
  You have a new guy every week!
KATY: Paul it's quite different when you *choose* to have a relationship with someone.
SUSY: A new partner would do *you* good Paul.
PAUL: I am perfectly happy!
SUSY: Paul, you're terrified. She's a dragon.
PAUL: I love her, Susy. Will you please show some respect for that fact. I love Rachel and we're going to get married.
KATY: Yow.
PAUL: I know a heterosexual marriage wouldn't appeal to you, Katy, so – [PAUL *and* KATY *speak simultaneously*] There's really no point.
KATY: [*simultaneously*] Oh Jesus, Paul!
  Quite frankly I don't care if you are my brother, if you're going to continually criticise my lifestyle just don't bother coming round!
PAUL: I just think you should take into account how much it worries Dad!

ACT ONE

KATY: I don't give a stuff what he thinks! It's none of his business!

PAUL: He's very, very worried.

KATY: It's not Dad who's worried. He's too drunk to be worried about much these days –

[PAUL *protests.*]

It's you and Rachel who're worried – well not so much worried as embarrassed that your sister, the dyke, might turn up at your wedding!

[PAUL *protests.*]

Tell Rachel not to worry. I won't come. I'll just send you a wedding present. Does she have Amy Coulter's book, *Beyond the Phallus*?

PAUL: I really find it hard to understand the basis on which you both ridicule Rachel and I. We've both patently made something of our lives and all you two can boast is taxi driving and trying to rip off an employer!

SUSY: I am *not* trying to rip off an employer. I was humiliated and degraded for seven months and then fired! I'm entitled to everything I'm going to get.

PAUL: So what happened? Exactly?

SUSY: Exactly? My boss made at least one phone call a day which suggested things like I come to his office, take off my clothes and suck his cock!

PAUL: These things only happen if they're encouraged.

[*The two sisters howl at him.* PAUL *loses his temper.*]

The clothes you wear. The short dresses. What kind of signals does that send?

SUSY: You want women to dress like Muslims. Covered from head to foot?

KATY: [*simultaneously*] Women are only raped because they provoke it?

PAUL: No one ever phones up Rachel at her work and suggests things like that, and maybe it's because she doesn't wear dresses with her breasts almost popping out!

SUSY: Rachel hasn't *got* any breasts!

PAUL: Why do you feel so superior, Susy? Why do you feel entitled to ridicule Rachel and I.
SUSY: Because you're so pompous, smug and self satisfied.
KATY: And you're boring!
PAUL: And we've found God?
KATY: There's no God!
PAUL: How can you say that!
KATY: Because if there was, God'd be intelligent enough not to recruit you two!
PAUL: There was a purpose for my visit today, but if all you're going to do is hurl insults at me I guess I'd better go.
KATY: Paul, I'm sorry. But sometimes you're so – heavy.
PAUL: Yeah, well Dad is very upset, and yeah, I am too. Especially now that Susy's lost her job.
SUSY: I'm fine Paul. I'm going to get forty thousand bucks.
PAUL: Forty thousand?
SUSY: He made my life hell!
PAUL: OK, but forty thousand bucks?
KATY: Harassment is just one step down from rape, Paul. Some women are so badly traumatised they need intensive psychiatric help just to get them functioning again.
PAUL: I just don't think –
SUSY: Paul, ask Rachel how she'd feel if it happened to her. Day in, day out. And she asked them to stop time and time again and they wouldn't. Ask her.
KATY: Paul, deep down we need to feel people are basically decent, and that if you ask them to stop doing something they know is really upsetting you they'll stop. When they don't it strips away your whole faith in human decency.
PAUL: I'm sorry but I really haven't noticed Susy being too traumatised in the last seven months. She's out every night.
SUSY: When there was shit going on every day, I had to.
PAUL: If you get that sort of money, what are you going to do?

Lies Lies Lies Lies Lies Lies Lies Lies Lies

SUSY: Start up a business.
PAUL: What kind of business.
SUSY: A coffee shop cum brasserie. Best fresh food, top location, top ambience.
PAUL: You can't even add up a column of figures.
SUSY: Katy's going to be my partner.
KATY: [*surprised, then recovering*] So tell Dad he needn't worry. Not that he'd ever care.
PAUL: Why do you keep saying he doesn't care?
KATY: Paul, face up to it. He's a drunk.
PAUL: He wasn't always a drunk, was he?
KATY: Yes, he was always a drunk, but he used to be a rich drunk and they're called 'colourful' or 'fun loving'.
PAUL: You weren't so derisive about him when he was sending you to top private schools, or expensive holidays, or off to Europe for two years with your own gold American Express cards, – I didn't hear much criticism of him in those days.

[*The two sisters look at each other, a little guiltily.*]

Look, I'm not trying to be heavy and 'Christian' about this, but Dad is a terribly sad guy right now, and when I talked to him the other night I felt really bad and remembered all the good things he'd done for us. You know what a rotten cricketer I was, but there he was week after week waiting for me to bat at number ten and get bowled first ball, full of encouragement, full of warmth and consolation. Some guys that I went to school with never *saw* their Dads. Who picked you two up after school, took you to dances, watched you play netball – look we all know his faults – but there was a lot of love there too. And he feels now that you only ever were decent to him because he kept showering you with money and that you couldn't care less now he's broke.
KATY: [*guiltily*] That's not true, Paul. We're just very busy.
PAUL: It's his sixty-third birthday coming up next week. Do you know what would thrill him?

KATY: A blowsy tart and a bottle of Johnny Walker.
   [PAUL *glares at her.*]
   Sorry. Yes he was affectionate, and he did do all those things for us, but he also made us put up with a succession of his hideous girlfriends, who were invariably drunker than he was –
SUSY: And the first of them arrived on our doorstep two weeks after Mum died.
KATY: They were there before Mum died. He just didn't bring 'em home till then.
PAUL: How do you know that?
KATY: I heard them arguing about it once. I heard how upset she was.
PAUL: OK. We all know his faults.
KATY: [*sighing*] What do you want us to do?
PAUL: You know what would really thrill him. If you invited him here, to your house, to dinner, for his birthday. Wednesday week. He told me he'd never even seen where you lived.
   [SUSY *and* KATY *look at each other.*]
   You've never invited him, and he's too proud to ask.
KATY: All right. Fine. Will Rachel come?
PAUL: No, er she can't make it.
KATY: Of course. We can't ask Rachel to break bread with a lesbian.
PAUL: Her committee meets Wednesday night.
KATY: Lawyers for Christ? Do they get a quorum?
PAUL: The Christian Lawyers Fellowship. They have a hundred and eighty members.
KATY: Thanking God for Conveyancing? Sorry.
SUSY: [*to* KATY] I saw him smile.
PAUL: Believing in God doesn't mean you can't have a sense of humour.
KATY: I had a dream that heaven was a giant version of the Comedy Club and God was up there doing one liners.
PAUL: And of course God was a woman?

KATY: Yes, and she was gay.
 [*A taxi toots out of sight.*]
SUSY: I've got to go.
PAUL: Party?
SUSY: Meeting friends. See you next Wednesday.
 [*She kisses him affectionately and goes.*]
PAUL: Katy, I just want to say that just because I have reservations about your lifestyle doesn't mean that I don't care about you. Or Susy.
KATY: I know. And we care about you. And Dad.
PAUL: I know it isn't very sexy in your eyes to be involved in floor coverings –
KATY: Paul, I don't – [*have any worries*]
PAUL: [*a glint in his eye, determined to be heard*] But some people have got to do the hard work of getting food on your tables, petrol in your car, and carpets in your hallways!
KATY: I know, Paul, I – [*know*]
PAUL: If everything comes together in the next year or so I'll have repaid my debt and be the owner of a thriving business.
KATY: Great.
PAUL: It wouldn't mean much to you or Susy but I'm already the second largest wholesaler of sea grass matting in the state.
KATY: Well done.
PAUL: Thank you. I know you don't mean it, but thank you. Does Susy really think she's going to rip forty thousand off her employer?
KATY: I believe her story, Paul. I believe she *was* unfairly dismissed and she *was* harassed.
PAUL: Really?
KATY: Severely harassed.
PAUL: Forty thousand dollars worth?

* * *

ACT ONE   17

The conference room. MARION *is there with* SUSY. *She is wearing a brighter and more flamboyant dress than last time.*

SUSY: Love your dress.
MARION: My husband says it makes me look like a bimbo.
SUSY: You look great.
MARION: The truth is I think he likes me looking like a bimbo. Twenty years after the feminist revolution and they still haven't changed.
SUSY: I think for a lot of men the revolution went – [*making an over-the-top-of-the-head gesture*] – unnoticed.
MARION: For quite a few women too. Gary denied everything.
SUSY: He's scarcely going to admit it.
MARION: If the harassment was upsetting you I presume you were applying for other jobs?
SUSY: No. I'd just been through all the hassle of trying to get a job. I knew how hard it was going to be to find another one.
MARION: If you weren't making any attempt to find another job it could seem as if the harassment wasn't worrying you.
SUSY: I knew it was no use applying for another job until I'd had some experience in this one. Leave a job after a few months and it's not going to look good on your record is it?
MARION: Vince and Gary both seemed to feel your work performance wasn't good.
SUSY: That's rubbish.
MARION: You were efficient?
SUSY: I was as efficient as I had to be. All I had to do was answer their phones and type a few letters and enter stuff on the spreadsheet.
MARION: You didn't spend a lot of time making personal calls, falling asleep at your desk, boasting about drug parties to married women?
SUSY: [*angrily*] Oh shit! Did they say that? Once or twice at

the most I came in a bit hung over. Occasionally I made a private call. Drugs? What drugs?
MARION: Ecstasy?
SUSY: I *knew* I shouldn't have told that mousy little suck. Once. I took it once, it did nothing for me and it's none of their business!
MARION: Vince did admit you did brighten the place up and that you could write a good letter.
SUSY: I was fine. They fired me because I wouldn't go down on Gary. End of story. They humiliated me and I want compensation!
MARION: I've scheduled a conference with them for next Thursday at three. Is that OK.
SUSY: Fine by me.
MARION: Can your sister come too.
SUSY: [*sharply*] Do we need her?
MARION: She's the only one who can corroborate your story.
SUSY: I'll ask her.

* * *

The office gymnasium. GARY *is working out watched by* VINCE.

GARY: I'm so bloody angry with that bitch.
VINCE: No one will believe her.
GARY: Vince, a large percentage of our population will be *delighted* to believe her. According to the feminists we're all rapists. Some of us just haven't got round to doing it yet.
VINCE: Come on. No woman I know believes that feminist rubbish.
GARY: Listen to Radio National some time, Vince. Sexual harassment, land rights, Affirmative Action and Multiculturalism. Our moral agenda is being dictated by Gay Armenians and Lesbian Turks. It's been open season

ACT ONE 19

on Anglo Celtic males for the last twenty years.
VINCE: But if you didn't do it —
GARY: Whoever said the world was fair?
VINCE: It's outrageous.
GARY: It's Australia in the nineties. The thought police have won. You don't have to have evidence, you just have to be able to lie. We're white wealthy males. Forget the fact that my parents were dirt poor, that I went to a lousy school, that I worked as a barman and studied till two o'clock in the morning to get my diploma. Forget all that. I'm a white middle class male, so I had it easy, so I'm fair game. It's Australia in the nineties.
VINCE: [*shaking his head*] It's very, very sad. This used to be the greatest country in the world. What happened?
GARY: We blinked, the trendies took over, and goodbye Australia. Vince, if it goes to court the press would be onto it immediately.
VINCE: [*nodding*] Stephanie would be devastated.
GARY: My wife is never *devastated*. That's far too passive. It's always somewhere between cold fury and blind rage. We've got to settle.
VINCE: Stephanie would be upset but I'm sure she wouldn't believe the allegations.
GARY: Oh yes she would. I've given her no cause to doubt me from the start of our marriage, but Stephanie still believes I would be capable of having sex with just about any animal you care to name.
VINCE: Gary, I think you'd find she trusts you more than you think.
GARY: Vince, I am married to the woman. If she wasn't the mother of my children I'd pay someone to feed her slowly into a mincer. And record her dying screams.
VINCE: I'm sure she wouldn't believe it.
GARY: Vince, let's talk straight here. You keep saying no one will believe it, but it took me half an hour to convince *you* Susy was lying.

VINCE: [*uneasily*] You haven't always behaved very well to the girls here, Gary.
GARY: Who exactly are you talking about Vince? Rhonda?
VINCE: I did overhear some things you said –
GARY: I was paying her compliments. If Rhonda's so flaky she leaves because I pay her a few compliments, then that's her problem.
VINCE: Let's not go into this again.
GARY: Whatever settlement we come to I assume the firm will cover me.
VINCE: [*uneasily*] How much money will she ask for?
PAUL: A lot.
VINCE: Five thousand?
GARY: Vince, they'll laugh at that. Vince, you owe me. I've kept this place from going under.
VINCE: *I've* been around here too, Gary.
GARY: Vince, *I* can't pay what they're going to want!
VINCE: Let's *ask* how much they want.
GARY: It's going to be more than five thousand. I can tell you that.
VINCE: Gerry said he saw you having lunch with two merchant bankers on Tuesday.
GARY: Couple of old college friends, Vince.
VINCE: Ah. I thought that was probably it.
GARY: I expect the firm to cover me, Vince.
VINCE: I can't promise anything till I find out what they want.

* * *

KATY *and* SUSY's *apartment.* KATY *stands there. She does not look happy.* SUSY *walks in in a dressing gown, barely awake.*

KATY: You could've at least done the dishes. What is this new routine? No work so you sleep in till midday?
SUSY: What are you doing home at this hour?
KATY: I got a job in the area so I thought I'd drop in and

maybe say hi, and have a cup of coffee, and maybe hear a few odd words of appreciation like, 'Gee Katy you look really tired. I really appreciate the way you work twelve hours a day to keep the both of us alive'.
SUSY: Gee Katy you look really tired. I really appreciate –
[KATE *whacks her on the arm to stop her.*]
You want coffee?
KATY: No, I'm drinking too much of it.
SUSY: So, hi.
[*She sits down opposite* KATY *and looks at her.*]
KATY: How come I wear that gown and look like a polar bear, and you wear it and look . . much better than I look.
SUSY: [*giving her an exaggerated smouldering look*] Because I am a Sex Goddess. If I'd been born in America I'd be Madonna by now.
KATY: We could do with the money. I've made less than a hundred and fifty dollars and it's Wednesday. So how did your meeting go?
SUSY: Good. She thinks I've got a great case for compensation.
KATY: I should think so.
SUSY: She wants you to come to the conference.
KATY: Why do I have to be there?
SUSY: Because I gave you a day by day account of the trauma Gary was causing me.
KATY: No, you didn't.
SUSY: I think your memory is faulty, Katy.
KATY: You want me to lie? I've got to go and lie?
SUSY: You're my only corroborating witness.
KATY: Shit, Susy.
SUSY: I was distressed. Remember?
KATY: Why *didn't* you tell me? If it's been going on seven months, why didn't you tell me?
SUSY: Because he was such a – geek – I was ashamed I couldn't handle it.
[KATY *looks at her.*]

KATY: So tell me what I'm supposed to remember.
SUSY: How I'd come home crying, desperate.
KATY: So why didn't I ring up and blast them? Lesbian feminists are supposed to do those things. Not to mention older sisters.
SUSY: They don't know you're a feminist lesbian – and I would appreciate it if you did everything in your power to conceal that fact –
KATY: You want me to lie at all levels.
SUSY: Certainly at that one.
KATY: What do you mean, certainly at that one!
SUSY: When you start on female issues, it can be some time before you stop.
KATY: When a man does it it's 'putting his case forcefully'. When I do it I'm 'totally out of control'.
SUSY: When a man does it it's two octaves lower.
   [KATY *looks at her disapprovingly.*]
KATY: I wish you hadn't brought me into this.
SUSY: I just felt that if I didn't have *someone* to back me up *no* one would believe me.
KATY: Susy, I hate telling lies. I'm no good at it.
SUSY: OK, don't come. Leave me with no hope.
KATY: Jesus you're a rat.
   [*Pause*]
Did you ever *really* feel distressed at what he was doing?
SUSY: [*emphatically*] Yes! I'm not lying about that!
   [*Pause*]
KATY: I hope you're going to do your share of the cooking for our father's birthday.
SUSY: Oh shit. When's that?
KATY: Try tonight.
SUSY: Have you got him a present?
KATY: Yes.
SUSY: Is it expensive enough that it could have been from both of us?
KATY: It's a tie.

SUSY: Oh shit. We always give him one each.
KATY: Then go and get him one.
SUSY: It's Sarah's party tonight.
KATY: Susy, you are staying home and entertaining your father. And you are helping me cook! Now go and buy a bloody tie!
SUSY: Can you lend me some money?
KATY: [*sighing*] Susy, you're going to need to get forty thousand just to pay back what you owe. [*Fishing in her pocket she pulls out a fifty dollar note*] There are some silk ones reduced from sixty dollars to twenty in DJ's.
SUSY: Where –
KATY: Can't miss 'em. They look like they've been designed by a Balinese on LSD. Dad'll love em. Don't get green. I got green. And mince and eggplants and cheap cheese. And a cask of red wine. I've kept some Wolf Blass bottles we can decant it into. Dad's taste buds gave out years ago.

* * *

It is evening at SUSY'*s apartment.* BRIAN, KATY, SUSY *and* PAUL *are there.* BRIAN *is a still handsome man of sixty-three who has been drinking too much and is slightly slurring his words. The dinner is over and* BRIAN *has taken himself off to the room's only armchair and is savouring a glass of red wine. He picks up the bottle and reads the label.*

BRIAN: Wolf Blass Grey label. It gets better and better and better. The man is a genius. Done more for the Australian wine industry than any other man. A bloody genius.
    [SUSY *and* KATY *look at each other.* PAUL *tastes his red wine and frowns.*]
PAUL: I think it's very disappointing. Very bland. I've tasted better wines than this in casks.
BRIAN: Paul, you're such a bloody know all!
PAUL: If you don't want me to have an opinion I won't.

BRIAN: It's a bloody good wine, and your sisters have spent a lot of money on it. Why do you always have to be so hypercritical.

PAUL: I'm entitled to my opinion.

BRIAN: Yeah, well your opinion is usually worth shit, so shut up.

PAUL: Fine.

BRIAN: You're a good kid mate, but your one fault – your one fault, is that you're a bloody know all.

PAUL: Fine.

BRIAN: Listen. Paul. You're a great kid. I love you as much as I love your sisters, but sometimes you're bloody irritating.

PAUL: Fine.

BRIAN: I just want to say something to all of you. This dinner tonight means more to me than you could possibly, possibly imagine. I once had the lot. More money than I knew what to do with, a loving wife, wonderful kids. Then fate intervened and took your mother in the cruellest possible way. We watched her fade away and die. In appalling pain. If I'd been a stronger, better person I would have gained strength from this loss. But instead of that I sank into a morass of self pity and self indulgence. I slept with women who weren't a tenth the person your mother was. I drank and I did what no salesman should ever do. I started to believe my own bullshit. I started to believe I could pick the trends on the property market a year before they happened. Instead of being content to sell properties and pocket the commission, I started to buy properties myself. I couldn't pick the market. The crash came a year before I thought it would and now I'm bankrupt, barred from practicing my trade, and living in a tiny one bedroom flat opposite a tiny, grubby little park, and I've only got myself to blame. All I've got left is you guys. And sometimes I think I've even lost you.

PAUL: You haven't.

BRIAN: If I did, Paul. I'd shoot myself. Because you guys are all I've got left. All. All. I know you're mad at me, and so you should be. I should have had millions to leave you, millions.
  [*They protest that this is not an issue.*]
  Twenty-three million on paper at one stage.
SUSY: Twenty-three million?
BRIAN: And now I'm a penniless drunk. And I know you're mad at me for that.
SUSY: Twenty-three million?
BRIAN: Twenty-three million. Isn't that bloody amazing. A kid who had to wear shoes with holes in them because his parents couldn't afford any more. Twenty-three million.
SUSY: You blew twenty-three million?
BRIAN: Twenty-three million.   *Susy cares too much obvious for herself.*
SUSY: Dad, you're a fucking idiot!
PAUL: Susy.
SUSY: Well, he is. He's an idiot!
BRIAN: I know you're all mad at me. You've got a right to be.
  [SUSY *gets up and goes for her handbag.*]
SUSY: I've got to go. One of my friends is having her engagement party.
KATY: Susy!
SUSY: Just shut up.
BRIAN: Let her go.
SUSY: He *is* a fucking idiot.
KATY: Susy, don't be such a bitch.
SUSY: Sorry. I'm out of here.
  [*She goes, slamming the door. There is a silence.*]
PAUL: That is absolutely typical.
KATY: Paul. Shut up.
BRIAN: I can understand it. It's not the money. It's just that it would've protected her from indignities like having to work for that slime who propositioned her. She's better than that.
PAUL: Why is she better than that? We all have to earn a

living. The only profession that pays money for a pretty face is prostitution.
BRIAN: Some people have a quality of – magic – about them. You can't say why. She's got it. She'll do something that'll surprise us all one day.
KATY: Magic?
BRIAN: Katy, Katy, Katy. Your magic is your creativity. Those designs you did. Breathtaking.
KATY: So breathtaking I was the first laid off when my firm made cuts.
BRIAN: Maybe there were other reasons.
KATY: Of course there were other reasons. It's an almost totally all male firm and they found out I was a dyke.
BRIAN: I have to say this Katy – I think I'd be failing as a father if I didn't – I do happen to think you've taken a wrong turn. Men are men and women are women for a purpose.
KATY: Oh God.
BRIAN: Katy, hear me out. I think there is a – profound magic – in that indefinable and mysterious difference between man and woman. A mystery that kept me tantalised and intrigued by your mother to her dying day.
KATY: Dad, sometimes you speak such shit I just can't take it any more. You were screwing drunken sluts for years while Mum was still alive. It drove her crazy.
BRIAN: [*long sigh*] That, to me is one of the deepest mysteries. How could a man who loved a woman like I loved your mother do that? It's a question I'm still asking myself every day of my life.
KATY: You know something, Dad. The question I'm still asking *myself*, birthday and all –
PAUL: Don't Katy. Please.
KATY: – is what kind of temporary insanity caused our mother to marry you.
PAUL: Katy.
KATY: Did you have charisma once? After the wedding did a

Lies Lies Lies Lies Lies Lies Lies Lies

horse kick you in the head? If Mum *had* to go and get herself married, why you?

BRIAN: [*sighing, then to* PAUL] She's right. There were much better men than I was chasing her. Much better. Why me? Again, it's one of those profound mysteries in the dance of the sexes. A dance, Katy, that I am really, really sad you're going to miss.

KATY: Dad, if the dance of the sexes meant I might end up with someone like you, I know why I sat it out.

[*She gets up with the dishes and moves noisily to the kitchen.* BRIAN *watches her go and turns to* PAUL.]

BRIAN: Should I just accept the fact she sleeps with women? Say nothing?

PAUL: No, you're absolutely right. If you ask me, all this 'gayness' is nothing more than a fashionable pose. An easy way out. A relationship with the opposite sex is difficult, but ultimately far more rewarding.

BRIAN: Absolutely. Male and Female. Drifting alien continents, forced to lock and learn each other's secrets. Gayness is just narcissism. Falling in love with one's own image. Shallow and vain.

[*Pause*]

Thank God Susy stayed straight.

PAUL: Wouldn't 'promiscuous' be more accurate?

BRIAN: That girl will surprise us one day.

PAUL: If she rips forty thousand off her employer I think it's scandalous.

BRIAN: We don't know what happened, Paul.

PAUL: [*agitated*] How can she claim harassment. She dresses like a tart, Dad. An absolute tart. She's asking for it!

BRIAN: [*shrugging*] Not like a tart. Much better taste.

PAUL: I've worked my guts out for every dollar I've ever earned and she finally gets a few months work then tries to rip the system off! Aren't you a little bit outraged?

BRIAN: Don't be so judgemental, Paul.

PAUL: I'm judgmental, I'm a know all. Anything else you'd like to call me?
BRIAN: You're a good kid. You're making something of your life. We've all got faults.
PAUL: I can't fathom you, Dad.
BRIAN: What have I done?
PAUL: *I* organised tonight. I had to drag them kicking and screaming to get them to invite you here. You're big enough to admit that you blew it financially, and Susy walks out. You're honest enough to tell Katy you don't approve of her gayness, and *she* storms out, but I'm judgemental and I'm a know all! Come on. I'll drive you home.
BRIAN: Son, you're just as important to me as they are.
PAUL: Yeah. They treat you like shit. They spit in your face and you come back for more!
BRIAN: [*shrugging*] Fathers and daughters. There's always a bit of a thing there.
PAUL: They do come first, You admit it.
BRIAN: Jesus, Paul!
PAUL: Don't say that.
BRIAN: What?
PAUL: Jesus!
BRIAN: Jesus! You know what the *most* disappointing thing in my life is? That you've become a bloody Christian!
PAUL: Dad –
BRIAN: How could *anyone* believe that this appalling, bruising, humiliating, state of interpersonal warfare we laughingly call *life* is designed by an all loving father! Shit!
PAUL: I'm sorry, but I do so choose to believe.
BRIAN: 'I do so choose to believe.' The kid I knew would never use language as stilted and anal as that!
PAUL: [*vulnerable, almost on the point of tears of desperation*] I have to believe in *something*! Rachel says you don't have to believe in a stupid fairytale God who

watches all our destinies. Perhaps God is just the force that started the Big Bang, but there's got to be some order, some purpose, otherwise what's the bloody point!

> [BRIAN *puts his arm around his son's shoulder in a genuinely warm and comforting gesture. We can suddenly see the father who consoled his son through the endless sporting failures of his youth.*]

BRIAN: Sorry son. It's me who's the judgemental old bastard. If it helps you to believe, believe. Don't listen to worn out old sods like me who've got one foot in the grave.

PAUL: Have you been to the doctor yet?

BRIAN: I'm fine.

PAUL: You're not. If you're getting chest pains every time you exert yourself the chances are you've got heart problems.

BRIAN: If I die, I die. What the hell.

PAUL: Go on Monday. Right?

BRIAN: OK.

> [BRIAN *turns towards the kitchen.*]

Katy!

> [KATY *appears at the doorway.*]

I'm sorry. Considering how I've spent my life I've no business being judgemental about anyone elses. Thank you so much for the dinner. And the wine. I'm going to write a fan letter to Wolf Blass. Thank you.

> [BRIAN *holds out his arms, inviting an embrace.* KATY *hesitates, but then goes and embraces her father with warmth.*]

KATY: Paul says you've been getting pains. Go to the doctor.

BRIAN: On Monday, I promise. Monday.

PAUL: Thanks, Katy.

> [PAUL *gives her an awkward kiss, and* KATY *watches as* PAUL *and her father leave.* BRIAN *turns to give her a last cheerful wave.*]

* * *

ACT ONE 31

The conference room. MARION *sits in a single chair. On one side of her on a two-seater sit* SUSY *and* KATY. *On the other side,* VINCE *and* GARY.

MARION: First of all, this is not a court of law. This is an attempt at conciliating the problem through to an outcome that's satisfactory to both parties.
GARY: Can I ask a question?
MARION: Sure.
GARY: Who is she?
KATY: 'She' is Susy's sister.
GARY: Excuse me, but why is Susy's sister here?
MARION: Susy told her sister what was happening to her at work. She's here to corroborate Susy's story.
GARY: Her *sister?* How fair is that?
MARION: You can question Katy's version. That's your prerogative.
GARY: Her sister?
KATY: Being her sister doesn't automatically make me a liar!
VINCE: Can I just say at the outset that we're both very upset at the way we've been dragged in here as if we're criminals. Gary and I are men of substantial standing in the business community, and – [VINCE *and* KATY *speak simultaneously*] We don't feel it's –
KATY: [*simultaneously*] Substantial standing?
VINCE: What?
KATY: What are you trying to say? That two highly important men like you find it beneath your dignity to be called to account for a minor little thing like seven months of vicious sexual persecution?
GARY: Vicious sexual persecution?
VINCE: We don't feel it's right that unsubstantiated allegations...
KATY: [*to* VINCE] They're not unsubstantiated. I'm substantiating them!
GARY: Without sexual attraction the human race wouldn't

have survived, sweetheart! The death of sex means the death of man kind for Christsake!

KATY: [*to* GARY] I'm not saying you shouldn't *have* impulses. I'm just saying you should be mature enough to control them. And don't call me sweetheart!

GARY: I took a totally normal interest in an attractive woman and suddenly I'm a criminal!

KATY: After thousands of years of abuse, males are finally being held accountable, and you don't like it. Well let me tell you something *buster*, the days of automatic female deference to male power are over, and you just better get used to it!

MARION: There's no point in continuing if all we're going to do is to trade insults.

[*There is a silence.*]

KATY: Sorry.

VINCE: What's happened to this country? I grew up in an era where men and women were partners and friends.

KATY: And doctors had to prescribe huge quantities of valium to keep it that way.

MARION: [*packing up*] I think we'd better settle this in court.

KATY: Sorry, Marion. I really am.

VINCE: So am I. We *do* want this settled here.

MARION: [*hesitating, then unpacking*] Susy, you claim that Gary made phone calls of a sexual nature over seven months that you found distressing.

SUSY: Extremely distressing.

MARION: Given his behaviour, why did you agree to work back with him on the night of the alleged incident?

SUSY: We did have to get the new spreadsheet working and he said he was sorry. I didn't believe him, but if he tried anything I could at least do a 'but Gary, you *promised*'.

MARION: Why didn't you go to Vince before this if it was so upsetting?

SUSY: I like to think I can deal with my own problems myself.

MARION: But you did tell your sister?
SUSY: [nodding] Which in fact I normally don't. Which is some indication of how upset I was.
MARION: [to KATY] And Susy indicated to you how upsetting these phone calls were?
KATY: Yeah. Which is unusual for Susy. We're close in some ways but she does tend to keep her problems and worries to herself.
MARION: How upset did she indicate she was.
KATY: Very. Often she was in tears. That sort of thing.
GARY: Can I ask a question?
MARION: Of course.
GARY: [sarcastically] Thank you very much. Katy, it's obvious you're a feminist.
KATY: Do you always spit when you say that word?
GARY: Would a strong feminist whose sister came home crying with tales of brutal sexual exploitation just say to her, 'OK, just put up with it. It'll stop sooner or later.'
SUSY: Katy wanted to go down there and rip the place apart. I had to beg her to stop. [To Katy] Didn't I? I wanted to last out a year to show that I could stick at a job.
MARION: Katy?
KATY: I was very angry. But with the job market like it is, I could see Susy's point.
MARION: According to my notes, Susy alleges Gary grabbed her breasts from behind and said, [Reading] 'The twin peaks of womanhood. Soft, sweet, seductive', then you turned to see Gary's penis –
GARY: [angrily] Susy, that's bullshit. You know it is.
SUSY: That's exactly what happened.
GARY: It is utter, utter, utter, bullshit!
MARION: What did happen?
GARY: We'd been working an hour or two, she couldn't get the hang of it, she got up and said, 'Stuff this, I've got a party to get to'. I said, 'Look, this has *got* to be done'. And she said she wasn't being paid for it, and I said that

occasionally she had to be prepared to work back, and it developed into a shouting match and she stormed out. She obviously realised that she was finished at LifeOptions, so she hatched this bullshit story to screw money out of us.

VINCE: And she's not going to get away with it.

SUSY: You're lying, Gary. You know you are.

MARION: [*to* KATY] How did she describe the incident to you?

[KATY *does not hear the question. Her thoughts are elsewhere.*]

Katy, how did she describe the incident to you?

KATY: [*jolted back to the present*] Oh. Er. Exactly like she told you.

MARION: [*reading from notes*] He grabbed her breasts and said 'The twin peaks of womanhood. Soft –

KATY: [*interrupting*] Yes. All that.

GARY: She's lying too!

KATY: I'm not!

MARION: Please. Accusation and counter accusation isn't going to get us far.

GARY: Where is there to get? It's her word against mine and she's lying!

SUSY: I'm not!

GARY: Let's stop all this crap and start being realistic. I'm in a no win situation. If this goes to court I'm going to lose out even if I win. There'll be jokes behind my back for the rest of my life and my wife and kids will suffer. If I want to preserve my reputation I've got to pay money.

MARION: No one wants you to pay money if the charges are untrue.

GARY: How in the hell can we prove it, one way or the other! It comes down to who the jury likes the most. The system stinks!

VINCE: The cards are totally stacked.

GARY: Let's be totally realistic here, Marion. The system is stacked against me. I'm incredibly angry about that, but I'm also a realist. If we can give her her blood money and

settle this right here and now then I'm rational enough to realise that it's in my interest to do it that way. What kind of cash are we talking about?
SUSY: Forty thousand dollars.
[GARY *and* VINCE *stare at her. Even* MARION *looks surprised.*]
GARY: [*appealing to* MARION] That's insane.
MARION: It's a high figure but they're serious allegations.
SUSY: High figure? Why is it a high figure? Some football hero got three hundred and fifty thousand 'cause a magazine photographed his dick!
VINCE: Forty thousand is insane!
MARION: It's on the high side, but there are precedents.
SUSY: That's what I want or we go to court.
GARY: [*on the edge of panic*] This is coming from my pocket Susy. The firm's in debt. It can't pay. This is coming from my pocket.
SUSY: So it should. You're the one who did it!
GARY: Would it mean anything to you that I've got two small children, a mortgage you couldn't jump over and cash reserves of exactly two thousand dollars in the bank.
SUSY: It's not my problem.
GARY: There's no way you're going to get that out of me.
SUSY: Let's go to court and see what the jury thinks.
GARY: You've just blown it, honey.
SUSY: Don't call me honey!
GARY: I was prepared to play ball but not to the tune of forty thousand dollars.
SUSY: Suit yourself.
GARY: Just after I graduated I went to New York. By myself. First trip abroad. This guy came up and said he'd take my photo so I could send it home to the folks. Said the prints would arrive where I was staying the next day. Five bucks for four, ten bucks for ten. He took photos and just as I handed the ten bucks over I realised there was no film in the camera. The guy was a crook and mean as hell and

probably carrying a gun or a knife, but I wasn't going to let him get away with it. Not totally. I said I'll just have four prints. I insisted he give me five bucks change. He saw the look in my eye and gave me back five bucks.

SUSY: Forty thousand or we go to court.

GARY: You can rob me, but not forty.

VINCE: It's outrageous. [*To* MARION] Can't you see that it's outrageous?

SUSY: Vince, you know what he's like!

GARY: Ten, and that's it.

SUSY: Forty.

VINCE: We can make it tougher for you in court than you think. Party girl, drugs –

GARY: You won't come out looking good, believe me.

MARION: These kind of threats are really counterproductive.

KATY: [*vehemently*] Counter productive? They're disgusting! What has her party going got to do with anything! Do you think because she's had sex with more than one guy she's available to anyone? Even men she despises!

GARY: Despises? Yeah. I guess I didn't go to the right school. I don't have the right accent. I don't wear trendy clothes – terrible sins I admit but she's not getting forty thousand out of me because of that.

KATY: She despised you because of the way you behaved!

GARY: She despised me, Vince, the firm, and everyone who worked there, right from the minute she started. That's why she thinks she can rip us off! Well let me tell you both something. It's our sort of energy and enterprise that keeps this country going! There's no way she's getting forty thousand out of me!

MARION: I think the best thing we can do at this stage is to call a halt now and let you all go away and think about it.

SUSY: [*to* GARY] You can think all you like, but I'm not shifting one dollar. You poisoned every day of my life for seven months and if it hurts you financially, tough. You deserve it!

ACT ONE 37

GARY: You think I'm just some nothing who you can squash. You'll find out you're very wrong!
MARION: This is very, very counterproductive. Can we just stop right now. Stop totally. Say nothing. Just file out of the door separately and don't say anything more? Please.
[*There is a silence.* VINCE *and* GARY *look at each other and get up to go.* KATY *and* SUSY *get up too.*]
I'll schedule another meeting for next Thursday, and I'll try and think this through a little more fully so we can make some progress.
[*They all look at each other.*]
If I need any further clarification before then, I'll contact you.

* * *

KATY's *apartment.* SUSY *bursts in, full of energy.* KATY *is thoughtful.* SUSY *turns to* KATY.

SUSY: We've got 'em.
KATY: Yeah.
SUSY: Maybe we'll have to come down a little way from forty, but basically they're stuffed and they know it.
KATY: Yeah.
SUSY: Gary knows he's trapped.
[*She whoops with joy.*]
If we make a go of the Brasserie, then we don't have to put up with shits like that ever again. Ever again.
[KATY *sits down in the armchair.*]
What's wrong?
KATY: Those words you used? Where did you get them from?
SUSY: What words?
KATY: 'The twin peaks of womanhood. Soft, sweet, seductive.'
SUSY: Gary. That's what he said.
KATY: No he didn't.

SUSY: [*frowning*] Are you saying I'm a liar.
KATY: Gary didn't say that. Dad did.
   [SUSY *stares at her.*]
SUSY: You told me he never touched you.
KATY: He did.
SUSY: You told me I was lying.
KATY: I'm sorry. I couldn't handle it. It was like reliving what *I* went through.
SUSY: How old were you?
KATY: I don't want to talk about it.
SUSY: How old were you?
KATY: Thirteen.
SUSY: So was I. What did he do?
KATY: Same as you. It would start as a game of 'chasey' and he'd end up grabbing my breasts from behind. I hated being left alone with him.
SUSY: I finally went right off my brain. I screamed and hit him.
KATY: I just used to plead with him to stop.
SUSY: Why didn't you scream?
KATY: I was scared Mum might hear. I would've killed myself before I let her find out.
SUSY: Did he go do anything worse?
KATY: No. The groping was the worst.
SUSY: How many times did he do it?
KATY: I lost count.
SUSY: Jesus. And Paul beats us round the head for not wanting him to dinner.
   [*Pause*]
I was shattered when you told me I was lying.
KATY: I just couldn't handle it. I think part of me was relieved it wasn't happening to me any more. I'm sorry.
SUSY: It's OK. It was worse for you than me.
   [*There is a pause. They are both lost in their own thoughts.*]
KATY: Is the rest of the stuff about Gary lies?

ACT ONE

SUSY: I made up the 'twin peaks', but grabbing my breasts and the rest was *absolutely* true.
[KATY *looks at her sister.*]
Don't you believe me?
KATY: Susy, you don't tell the truth all that often.
SUSY: If you'd admitted to me that Dad had done it to you too, then –
KATY: [*guiltily*] I said I was sorry Susy...
SUSY: – then I would have trusted you with other things. I would have told you about Gary. When you left me stranded back then I thought, 'what's the use of telling the truth if nobody's ever going to believe me'!
KATY: Susy, don't try and dump that one on me! You're a compulsive liar. You always have been. You were lying when you were three. I can't believe it sometimes. I hear you on the phone swearing to some guy that he's the one and only love of your life and some other guy comes yawning out of your bedroom.
SUSY: You have to juggle a bit. Everyone does.
KATY: Everyone does not! Not like you do!
SUSY: I'm not lying about Gary. Believe me.
[*There is a pause.* KATY *stares straight ahead.*]
We're going to get a lot of money, Katy. We are. Believe me.

END OF ACT ONE

Act Two

SUSY *and* KATY's *apartment. They are listening to a worried* PAUL.

PAUL: I saw a video of his angiogram. I'm not a doctor, but you didn't have to be to see what was going on.

SUSY: What's an angiogram?

PAUL: An x-ray of the heart pumping. You see the blood going through the coronary arteries. Dad's coronary arteries are almost totally blocked. It's a wonder any blood is getting through at all. They're almost totally blocked.

KATY: So what's the prognosis?

PAUL: He either gets a triple bypass soon or he's dead.

SUSY: So he gets a triple bypass.

PAUL: Sure. In twelve to eighteen months. That's the waiting list.

SUSY: Waiting list? He's privately insured isn't he?

PAUL: No.

KATY: No?

PAUL: How could he be? He's living on the pension.

KATY: Will he last twelve months?

PAUL: Probably not.

KATY: Then its an emergency. They've got to treat him.

PAUL: There are hundreds of others in the same position. Haven't you read about the hospital queues? It's got to the state where if you're not insured, and you're not about to die tomorrow, you take your chances.

SUSY: Can't we pull some strings?

PAUL: What strings? Dad didn't have many friends when he had twenty-three million. How many do you think he's got now?

KATY: What are his chances? Of living the twelve months.

PAUL: His doctor says fifty fifty, but my feeling was that he was being optimistic.

ACT TWO

KATY: So how much does this operation cost?
PAUL: Thirty thousand.
SUSY: Thirty thousand?
PAUL: It's open heart surgery.
SUSY: Thirty thousand.
KATY: Can you loan it to him, Paul?
PAUL: Thirty thousand?
SUSY: You're always telling us how well you're doing.
PAUL: I thought *you* were about to get forty thousand.
SUSY: Oh no. That's for me. You're the one with money. You've made something of your life. Remember?
[PAUL *looks extremely uncomfortable.*]
PAUL: I'd help him if I could.
KATY: You can.
PAUL: I can't.
SUSY: What do you mean, you can't! Are you doing well or aren't you?
PAUL: I possibly will be. But not yet.
SUSY: Paul, according to you you've been carpeting half this city for the last ten years.
[*They look at him.*]
PAUL: Maybe in two, three years time I'll be in the clear, but it's a highly competitive area.
SUSY: Paul, come on. You could raise thirty thousand if you had to.
PAUL: Susy, I'm a hundred and twenty thousand in debt.
KATY: In debt?
SUSY: Your girlfriend's a highly paid lawyer.
PAUL: She's sunk twenty-five thousand into the business already. She's kept me afloat.
[*The sisters look at each other.*]
I know what you think of her, but if it wasn't for Rachel I'd be sleeping on a park bench.
KATY: How's he taking it?
PAUL: He's cracking hearty, but underneath he's worried sick.
SUSY: He's sixty-three, for God's sake. If I drink half as much

as he has and live to sixty-three I'll count myself lucky.
PAUL: You'll just let him die?
SUSY: He won't die. Doctors are always pessimistic.
PAUL: He's spent much more than thirty thousand on you.
SUSY: Guilt.
PAUL: Guilt for what?
SUSY: For being a shit of a father.
PAUL: You deride me for being a Christian, but at least I've got the capacity to forgive.
SUSY: You've got less to forgive.
PAUL: [*angrily*] Have I? Have I indeed? You two got all the affection. He admitted as much the other night. The special thing fathers have for daughters. Great. He came to a few sports matches but otherwise I was nothing. The joke of the family. The know all. The humourless one. Mr Judgemental. Worrybum. Mr Yawn. I know all the names you used to call me.
KATY: What's the prognosis if he has the operation?
PAUL: Possibly ten more years of life, but that's nothing compared with you two opening a trendy brasserie.
SUSY: He won't die, Paul!
KATY: You're sure the doctor was telling the truth. A fifty fifty chance?
PAUL: I think he was being optimistic. I saw the angiogram, and honestly its a miracle any blood gets through.
SUSY: You're just a drama queen Paul. You always have been.
PAUL: OK. Let him die.
SUSY: I've had enough of this shit. I'm going out.
PAUL: That's right. Whenever something difficult or hard to face happens, off to another party. You are so gutless and shallow!
SUSY: You're such a geek, Paul.
PAUL: Yeah, a geek as well. One day you're going to have to start judging things beyond the surface.
SUSY: [*going*] Paul, you're so boring!

[PAUL *tries to control his rage.*]
PAUL: Sometimes I could really kill her.
KATY: I've tried. She recovers.
PAUL: She could give Dad ten more years of life.
KATY: If she gets the forty thousand she'll give it, but my feeling is it's a fantasy. With luck she might end up with five or ten.
[PAUL *looks at* KATY.]
PAUL: Is she lying about the harassment?
KATY: I wish I knew. Doesn't believe Susy
PAUL: [*nodding*] Who knows. You remember how she used to steal money from me, from Dad, from anyone. I found my missing ten dollars under her pillow one time and she *still* swore she hadn't taken it.
KATY: And Dad believed her. 'If I'd taken it, Dad, would I have been stupid enough to hide it under *my* pillow?' I got the thrashing.
PAUL: She tells brilliant lies. Why do you let her stay here with you? ← where does the brilliance lie? - Development of her lie - getting Katy to lie
KATY: The last man she was with kicked her out and she had nowhere to go.
PAUL: She *said* she had nowhere to go.
KATY: [*nodding*] She wanted somewhere independent and rent free. You know that's why Margot moved out. Couldn't stand her.
PAUL: Who could.
KATY: Come on. She's our sister, and she's out of a job. And she's much more vulnerable than she lets on.
PAUL: Vulnerable? On the scale of vulnerability our sister falls somewhere between Bronwyn Bishop and a Rottweiler. When you're a hundred and twenty thousand dollars down, *that's* when you're vulnerable.
KATY: You're really that much in debt?
PAUL: [*nodding*] I topped my year in business school, but out in the real world I'm a joke. Somewhere there's an understanding
KATY: You're talking to a taxi driver.

PAUL: To succeed in business you've got to be an utter bastard with no conscience, no compassion and no remorse. The guys that make it in my game quote on a certain type of carpet and deliver an inferior one and if they're questioned they put on such a brilliant act. 'You think I'd cheat you? Please. Ring up the manufacturer. Quote the batch number. Let's get this thing checked out.' Of course ninety-nine percent of customers never do because they're too embarrassed. I tried it once and couldn't go through with it.
KATY: I got a job designing a house three months ago. They ripped off my ideas and didn't pay me.
PAUL: My business lecturers used to say, 'It's jungle out there'. The predators in this city would scare the hell out of anything you'd find in a jungle.

    [*Pause*]

I'd pay the money for Dad if I had it. I really would.
KATY: So would I.

    [*Pause*]

I don't know why.

* * *

The conference room.

MARION: Thanks for coming in. I thought it might be useful if we talked a little before tomorrow's conference.
KATY: I don't think I can really add much more than I've already said.

    [MARION *looks at* KATY. *There is a pause.*]

MARION: I'm as cynical as anyone else about good triumphing over evil and all that, but most of the time I really feel the job I do here is worthwhile.
KATY: I'm sure it is.
MARION: I see it most of the time as helping the powerless to stand up to the powerful, and get some sort of justice. And

ACT TWO 45

if we're talking powerless, we're usually talking about women.

KATY: Don't I know it.

MARION: I get a lot of harassment cases in here and in almost every case I'm totally convinced that the woman involved has been put through a vicious and degrading humiliation. I try and stay neutral, but the truth is I'm usually on their side, and I think I should be.

[KATY *and* MARION *look at each other.* KATY *stays silent. She knows what is coming.*]

I'm becoming increasingly doubtful that your sister *has* suffered a vicious and degrading humiliation, and I don't like to think that this office is being used for fraudulent extortion.

KATY: Why do you –

MARION: It took a lot of effort to get this board started. The reactionaries tried everything they could to stop it. Anyone who misuses it gives them wonderful ammunition.

KATY: Why do you think my sister's lying?

MARION: You become quite good at interpreting body language in this job, and you looked very uncomfortable when you had to back up her story.

[KATY *is silent.*]

I can't say I particularly like Gary. In fact it would be nearer to the truth to say I can't stand him, but it seems to me that your sister has decided on a sum of money she wants and has manufactured her story to match it.

[KATY *remains silent.*]

I may be wrong, but I felt very strongly that I should voice my concerns to you before tomorrow.

[KATY *becomes agitated as she struggles with her conscience.*]

KATY: It sort of puts me in an impossible situation. Can we consider what I'm about to say totally confidential?

MARION: I don't think I can really give you that sort of guarantee.

KATY: Then I can't really say anything.
MARION: It's up to you.
> [KATY *becomes extremely uncomfortable. The silence holds for some seconds.*]

KATY: I *was* lying. Susy didn't tell me anything, but that doesn't necessarily mean she's lying about the harassment. She never tells me anything that's worrying her. She's not the confiding type.
MARION: Do you think she *is* lying?
KATY: I suspect she's exaggerating the office incident, but the phone calls – I don't think so.
> [KATY *looks uncomfortable.*]

MARION: Does she realise that if she pushes Gary too hard, he's just as likely to take this to court?
KATY: What about the publicity?
MARION: He'd prefer to avoid the publicity but if the alternative is forty thousand dollars . . .
KATY: [*concerned*] You think?
MARION: Yes, and their lawyer would make sure the jury heard that she parties, takes drugs, sleeps at work – I wouldn't like her chances. She could end up with nothing.
KATY: I'll talk to her.
MARION: I think you should.
> [*The two women look at each other.*]

Thanks for being so truthful Katy. It doesn't happen enough these days.
KATY: I think you're doing a fabulous job, and I'd hate to think Susy was ... yeah. I think you're doing a fabulous job.
MARION: Thank you.
> [KATY, *embarrassed that she might have revealed her attraction to* MARION, *retreats.*]

* * *

KATY's *place.* SUSY *stares at her.* SUSY *is angry.*

KATY: It's too much!
SUSY: It's what we need!
KATY: You'll blow it Susy. It'll backfire.
SUSY: Don't wimp out. This is for both of us.
KATY: I told her I lied.
SUSY: [*staring at her*] What!
KATY: She spotted it. She knew I was lying.
SUSY: Shit, Katy. You're a wimp!
KATY: I told her I still believed you were telling the truth.
SUSY: Great!
KATY: I couldn't lie!
SUSY: [*parodying her*] I couldn't lie. I couldn't lie. God you're a fucking Pollyanna. You'll be driving a taxi all the rest of your stupid life!
KATY: I couldn't lie to her!
SUSY: As soon as I saw that dyke I knew you'd fall in love with her!
KATY: Marion?
SUSY: Yes, Marion!
KATY: She's not gay.
SUSY: Get new glasses. She was eyeing you all through the conference.
KATY: Really?
SUSY: God you're a loser, Katy. You can't even spot your own species! Don't you know that every female lawyer in Sydney is gay, except Christian bloody Rachel! Now she's going to think I'm a total liar!
KATY: I told her I thought you were telling the truth.
SUSY: I was! Gary was vile to me for nearly seven months, and I hated every minute of it, and he's going to pay forty thousand.
KATY: Marion says he won't pay. He'll go to court.

SUSY: Yeah, well I know Gary Fitzgerald better than Marion does. He'd do anything to hide this from his wife and her family. He's terrified of them.
KATY: Susy, be reasonable.
SUSY: And live the rest of our lives like this? No way.

* * *

GARY's *office.* GARY *is furious.* VINCE *is defensive.*

GARY: So how much *will* the firm back me with, Vince. I need to know.
VINCE: Given the financial position the firm is in –
GARY: How much?
VINCE: If it does go to court it'll probably be just one tiny paragraph in the afternoon paper.
GARY: Vince! It'll be on *Sixty* bloody *Minutes*! It'd be a disaster for me. Stephanie and her whole bloody family will –
VINCE: Gary, you place too much store by what Stephanie and her family think.
GARY: I have to live with them.
VINCE: Her father's just a bloody dermatologist. What's so Godlike about a guy who cures itches! Take her to court.
GARY: There's another agenda here, Vince.
VINCE: What?
GARY: You're refusing to pay because you *do* believe her.
VINCE: I'm refusing to pay because the firm's broke!
GARY: You believe her.
VINCE: I don't!
GARY: You do or you wouldn't be prepared to see me crucified in court.
VINCE: Gary, the public will be on your side. A drug taking promiscuous party girl – she'll be crucified. You'll win.
GARY: You believe her so you're prepared to throw me to the wolves!

ACT TWO

VINCE: [*under strain*] The firm'll cover you for ten thousand. I think that's fair.

GARY: Well, I tell you something Vince. I don't. You're throwing me to the wolves!

VINCE: [*losing patience*] Gary, there has to be *some* truth in what she says!

GARY: Now it comes out!

VINCE: There *has* to be. Considering the way you've treated other women around the office.

GARY: A few jokes! A few compliments!

VINCE: I know you've had affairs with at least two of our girls...

GARY: They were willing. They wanted it! Vince, you're a fossil. They should carbon date you. Have you ever heard of Madonna? Most women love sex!

VINCE: Yeah, well why do they always leave? Ten thousand. I think that's more than fair.

GARY: I don't Vince. And I'm really pissed off.

[GARY *stares* VINCE *in the eyes.* VINCE *eventually looks away.*]

* * *

The conference room. MARION, SUSY, KATY, VINCE *and* GARY *are there. There is a lot of tension.*

SUSY: You're joking?

VINCE: It's our last and final offer.

SUSY: Ten thousand? You're joking.

VINCE: It's more than we ever intended and frankly we're outraged at having to pay it.

SUSY: You *want* this to go to court?

VINCE: If it has to.

SUSY: [*getting up, then turning to* MARION] Could you schedule the hearing as soon as possible?

GARY: OK. Ten of my own. A total of twenty.

VINCE: Gary.
GARY: I haven't got ten. I'm going to have to borrow so it's our absolute final offer. And let me tell you, you could not imagine how angry I am at having to do this. To say I think it's criminal would be grossly understating it. Twenty thousand. Final offer.
SUSY: [*to* MARION] Could you schedule the hearing as soon as possible?
GARY: I can't believe this!
VINCE: Susy, you can't be serious. Twenty thousand dollars. Ten of it straight from Gary's pocket!
MARION: Susy, twenty thousand is an offer I really think is worth considering seriously.
SUSY: I'm sorry. I don't think it's enough.
  [*The two women stare at each other.*]
VINCE: [*to* MARION] It's a very generous offer, isn't it?
MARION: It's within the range of what I consider fair.
SUSY: Marion, as I understand it this is a negotiation between Gary and me?
MARION: I'm just offering an opinion.
SUSY: In my opinion twenty thousand isn't nearly enough. Let's see what the tribunal thinks.
VINCE: [*to* SUSY] I would have thought that there were things you'd want to keep out of the media too.
SUSY: Like what?
VINCE: Like your lifestyle.
SUSY: I once took Ecstasy? Phwoar! I won't ever be able to show my face around Kinsela's again.
GARY: What *will* you take?
VINCE: Gary, don't let her do this to you!
GARY: What *will* you take?
SUSY: Forty thousand.
GARY: There is no way! Can't you understand? There is no way I could raise forty thousand even if I wanted to!
SUSY: What are your net assets, Gary? Way above forty thousand I suspect.

GARY: You want me to sell my house?
SUSY: If necessary. People go to prison for what you did. You're getting off lightly.
VINCE: [appealing to MARION] She's crazy. She's insane.
SUSY: [to VINCE] Vince, you know what he's like!
GARY: [to SUSY, desperately] For God's sake be reasonable.
SUSY: Were you reasonable to me?
GARY: Forty is fantasy land. What will you really take? The real figure.
SUSY: [sensing her power, enjoying it] I'm not budging Gary, forty.
GARY: [angrily] Don't be bloody stupid! Despite the fact I'm totally innocent I'm offering you extra out of my own pocket! Be bloody reasonable!
SUSY: When were you ever reasonable to me?
GARY: [angry almost to the point of tears of rage] I didn't do anything to you and you know it! How can you sit there and lie!
SUSY: I'm not lying Gary. You are.
   [GARY lets out a cry of pain and rage and gets up as if to strike her. He is restrained by VINCE.]
GARY: You're a bitch! You're a lying, vicious, filthy, rotten bitch!
VINCE: Gary!
SUSY: You're certainly not going to get out of it for less than forty now.
MARION: I'm sorry. That's the finish. The conference is over.
GARY: You bitch!
   [KATY has become progressively more agitated. She cannot take it any longer.]
KATY: We'll take the twenty!
SUSY: [turning on her] This is nothing to do with you!
GARY: [pointing to KATY] She knows it's bullshit! She knows!
MARION: Susy, this conference is over.
SUSY: I'll take thirty and that's it! That's absolutely it!

MARION: We're not striking any bargains today. The conference is over.
GARY: Let her have the thirty. As long as I never see the bitch again!
VINCE: Gary!
GARY: Give it to her! Vince, you do fifteen, I'll do fifteen.
MARION: The conference is over.
SUSY: This is between me and him!
GARY: You owe me Vince. You owe me!
MARION: No agreements. Not today.
SUSY: It's none of your business.
MARION: Susy, I set this process up. It runs to my rules.
GARY: Give her the money!
MARION: Gary, just go. Vince, take him with you.
VINCE: Gary, let's get out of here.

[GARY, *broken, turns and allows* VINCE *to lead him out of the room. There is a silence.* SUSY *turns on* MARION.]

SUSY: Thanks. Thanks a million. Why in the hell didn't you let them settle?
MARION: There can't be a balanced settlement under conditions like that.
SUSY: Marion, he wanted to pay! Why did you pull the plug?
MARION: Because quite frankly I don't believe your story's true. Any of it.
SUSY: What are you saying? I'm lying?
MARION: Yes. And I hate to see this whole process being abused this way. There are an awful lot of women who *really* suffer who need this board!

[*Pause*]

SUSY: You listen to me, *Marion.* I am not lying. He was on the phone every day saying things more degrading and hostile than you are ever likely to hear in your protected little life, so keep out of this!
MARION: You *did* lie about the office incident, didn't you!

ACT TWO

SUSY: It didn't happen *exactly* as I told it, so what! Whose side are you on!

> [*She turns on her heel and storms out.* MARION *and* KATY *stand there not saying anything for a second or two.* MARION *looks at* KATY. *There is a pause.*]

MARION: Does she realise how dangerous this is getting?

KATY: I think she thinks she's going to win.

> [*Pause*]

Would you like to go for a coffee?

MARION: [*looking at her watch*] It'd have to be quick. My husband's picking me up early.

KATY: Oh.

MARION: It's our wedding anniversary.

KATY: Congratulations. Excuse me. I've just got to go and kill someone.

* * *

GARY's *office. He is sitting there staring straight ahead.* VINCE *enters.*

GARY: She humiliated me. She made me panic.

VINCE: I think we have to call her bluff.

GARY: You don't have to do anything, Vince. *I* have to call her bluff.

VINCE: Good.

GARY: I've been behaving like a coward on all fronts.

VINCE: I think your reaction was totally understandable.

GARY: No, it was gutless. I've done what I should have done weeks ago. I've told Stephanie and her parents and they're right behind me.

VINCE: Good.

GARY: She's going to get nothing. She's got the mother of a fight on her hands.

VINCE: I'm really glad.

GARY: No one humiliates me like that and gets away with it. This's been a turning point for me, Vince.

VINCE: Good.

GARY: The public aren't stupid. They'll see this for what it is. A blatant attempt to extort money by a scheming amoral little bitch!

VINCE: I hope you understand why I couldn't go higher than ten.

GARY: Oh, I understand all right. You believe every word she says.

VINCE: That's not true.

GARY: [*nodding*] And that was a real shock. But it's freed me. If that's what you think of me then fuck you, Vince. Fuck you.

VINCE: Hey, now just a minute.

GARY: You believed her. So fuck you!

VINCE: [*struggling to get it out*] I've got reason to believe her. Good reason.

GARY: Oh yeah. What?

VINCE: I was looking at an advertising layout in the partition behind her desk one day and I heard her on the phone.

GARY: What did you hear?

VINCE: I heard her pleading with you to stop.

GARY: Stop what?

VINCE: Stop calling her. I heard what she said.

GARY: What?

VINCE: She said something like, 'Gary, please, please stop it. I don't mind a guy being angry, but you're sick'. And she was *very, very* upset.

GARY: If it had've been that bad she would've left.

VINCE: She said there was no way you were going to make her leave. And you know something, I admired her guts. That's why I didn't want to fire her. I *know* how you treat women around here.

[*There is a silence.* GARY *looks at* VINCE. VINCE *shifts uncomfortably.*]

Lies   Lies   Lies

Lies

Lies

Lies

Lies

Lies

Look you've done a good job here Gary. I'd be the first to admit that, but –
GARY: You want me to leave? Get out of here? Is that the message?
   [*Pause*]
VINCE: Yeah, Gary. Actually it is. I think when all this is settled it might be best if you moved on.
GARY: I've got a little bit of news for you Vince. As of today I've got two merchant banks backing a buyout of this joint. Only condition. I run it.
VINCE: Those merchant bankers you were having lunch with? They were supposed to be college friends.
GARY: I lied. Don't get pious Vince. This place was ripe for a management buyout. These are hard times. We've got to become much more aggressive and you know, and I know and they know that you haven't got the guts to go in hard.
   [*Pause*]
You can always refuse to sell. But if you do that I'll leave and you'll go bankrupt.
   [*Pause*]
VINCE: You know something? I'll be happy to go. I've been ashamed of the way we've been operating ever since you came.
GARY: Fuck you, Vince. I was the reason you survived.
VINCE: When I started this firm it really did give worthwhile advice to its clients.
GARY: Vince, I'm giving you a better price for this shit heap than anyone else will, so if the tribunal subpoena's you, think carefully about what you say.
VINCE: [*contemptuously*] You needn't worry, Gary. Vengeance isn't my cup of tea.

* * *

ACT TWO

KATY *and* SUSY *wait at a bus stop.* SUSY *is agitated.* KATY *looks grim.*

SUSY: If we withdraw the complaint we get nothing. Absolutely nothing!
KATY: Gary's going to court! I can't lie in court!
SUSY: You really fucked up, Katy. We had a way out and you really fucked up!
KATY: Get another job!
SUSY: And put up with that shit again. No way.
KATY: OK, starve!
SUSY: I can get married.
KATY: Try prostitution. It's more honest.
SUSY: There's nothing wrong with families.
KATY: No. Look at ours.
SUSY: Do we have to see Dad today?
KATY: Yes. He's expecting us!
SUSY: I'll take the twenty thousand.
KATY: Gary's withdrawn all offers.
SUSY: We'll take ten.
KATY: He's going to court.
SUSY: It's just a bluff.
    [KATY *sighs.*]
Can you lend me fifty bucks?
KATY: No.
SUSY: Stuff this. I will get married. Have kids.
KATY: Does the world really need more of your genes?
SUSY: Lend me twenty. The bloody machine swallowed my last credit card!
KATY: Susy, if I had money would we be here waiting for a bloody bus?

* * *

BRIAN's garden. BRIAN *sits in a deck chair looking haggard and unwell but still managing to radiate bonhomie and optimism, due partly to the fact that as usual he has been drinking.* PAUL *sits near him.* KATY *further away.* SUSY *patrols up and down restlessly.*

BRIAN: We're born, we prosper, we wither and we die. It's called the human condition.
PAUL: We're going to raise the money, Dad.
BRIAN: No you're not. The government's going to pay for this operation, not you.
PAUL: In twelve to eighteen months?
BRIAN: I'll last that long. God, I'm not that sick.
PAUL: I've spoken to the doctor. I've seen your angiograms.
BRIAN: I appreciate what you're saying, but I know the reality. I know how much debt you're in, Paul. And I know the girls haven't got any cash to spare.
PAUL: I'm going to get you to make me a list of all your old friends –
BRIAN: Save your energy.
PAUL: I'm sure they'd –
BRIAN: Paul, thank you, but during my life I have had something like two million acquaintances but no friends.
SUSY: I thought I was going to get some money off my employer, but it looks like –
BRIAN: Katy told me.
 [*There is a silence.*]
 You shouldn't even feel obligated. It's not as if I've been a great father.
PAUL: You've been terrific.
 [*There is a silence. No reaction from* KATY *and* SUSY.]
BRIAN: Thank you, girls.
KATY: [*guiltily*] Paul said it for all of us.
BRIAN: [*Sarcastically*] Thank you. Thank you for letting Paul speak on behalf of that great depth of warmth you both

feel for me. First time you've ever let him speak for you in his life.
SUSY: [*angrily*] Dad, you behaved like a shit. Most of the time you behaved like a shit. I'm sorry you're sick, but I can't suddenly lie that I think you're wonderful and all that crap.
PAUL: Susy.
BRIAN: [*Flaring*] *I* behaved like a shit! Jesus. How many times did I have to cover for you young lady. I had to go and beg your headmistress not to expel you, not once, not twice but three times! For stealing money off girls whose parents only had a fraction of what we had.
SUSY: Here we go again.
BRIAN: Why did you have to steal? I gave you more than enough money.
SUSY: Because I was bored!
PAUL: Calm down, Dad.
SUSY: If you were looking for excitement at my school the only thing on offer was an extra maths unit.
BRIAN: There were a *few* more things on offer I seem to remember. And you tried them all. Smoking, drinking, boys. Katy didn't give me anywhere *near* the trouble you did.
SUSY: No, Katy was much more compliant.
BRIAN: When I got the medical verdict I did have one quick moment thinking, 'Ah, Susy's getting forty thousand. Maybe all isn't lost'. Then I immediately came to my senses and knew there's no way Susy'd ever give it to me, even if it did mean ten years of life.
KATY: She would have given it to you, Dad.
SUSY: No, I bloody well wouldn't have!
PAUL: Why?
SUSY: He knows why.
KATY: Susy. Shut up.
BRIAN: If you'd offered I wouldn't have taken it. You've got a right to a decent start in life and I recognise that, but I

would like to think you might've offered!
KATY: Susy. The man is ill.
SUSY: He carries on with this act of hurt and wounded dignity.
BRIAN: I am hurt. Deeply hurt to think that you wouldn't even have offered. I've spent three times that amount on you in your life, young lady!
SUSY: Out of guilt!
BRIAN: Guilt for what?
KATY: [*pre-empting* SUSY] For being drunk so often. For having all those appalling women.
BRIAN: Appalling? Which ones were appalling?
KATY: All of them.
BRIAN: What about Gwen Mountjoy. She was like a mother to you.
KATY: Gwen Mountjoy couldn't find her way to the kitchen after five o'clock.
BRIAN: OK. None of them were as good as your mother.
SUSY: Dad, we'll try and raise the money somehow. We'll go round to all those acquaintances and screw something out of them. Just don't bullshit about being ready to die if you're not.
BRIAN: No one's ever quite ready to die.
SUSY: And don't put on that wounded act because we don't sit round your feet adoring you. There are reasons and you know what they are.
KATY: Susy. Just give it a rest, will you?
SUSY: [*to* KATY] Someone should say it!
BRIAN: What?
SUSY: That you're a sleaze!
KATY: Susy, no!
SUSY: He is.

   [BRIAN *stares at her.*]

BRIAN: [*looking shocked*] What are you saying, Susy?
SUSY: I'm saying you shouldn't be particularly surprised if we aren't as enthusiastic as we should be!

ACT TWO 61

BRIAN: Because I made a few innocent comments about the fact you were growing into young women?
PAUL: Susy, what the hell are you on about?
BRIAN: Is that what you're referring to?
KATY: Forget it, Dad.
BRIAN: I won't forget it! So your breasts grow. So I notice it and comment. Is this a hideous crime?
KATY: Let's not get too melodramatic.
BRIAN: Is this a hideous crime?
KATY: No. Can we forget it?
SUSY: That's right Katy. Sweep it under the carpet like last time.
BRIAN: All fathers notice their daughter's development. I was proud! All fathers notice.
SUSY: All fathers don't chase their daughters and grab their breasts!
BRIAN: Susy, I didn't!
KATY: Calm down! It happened. It shouldn't have happened, but I'm sure it hasn't totally ruined our lives.
SUSY: He just should understand why we're not prepared to cut off our right arms for him!
BRIAN: I didn't touch them, Paul. I swear!
SUSY: Dad, don't lie! You only stopped when I screamed at you. Even if alcohol has destroyed most of your brain, you *have* to remember that.

   [*There is a pause.* PAUL *looks acutely embarrassed.*]
BRIAN: I deserve to die.
KATY: Don't be so bloody melodramatic.
BRIAN: I deserve to die.
SUSY: Dad, don't start that.
KATY: You have got *some* redeeming features.
BRIAN: Name them.
KATY: When Mum got sick, you were gentle and you were kind.

   [*There is a silence.* PAUL *stares at the ground,*

shaking his head in disbelief. SUSY *bites her lip and moves closer to her father.*]

SUSY: [*to* BRIAN] I'm sorry. I shouldn't have dumped that on you. You've got enough problems. What is *wrong* with me?

KATY: On your bad days you're a psychopath, on your good days you're a shit.

PAUL: Susy, could I ask you not to mention this to Rachel?

KATY: Tell her Paul. We need her prayers.

BRIAN: No more talk of raising money. If I die, I die. I mean it.

KATY: Dad, please stop being penitent. Your remorse is more nauseating than your crimes!

[*There is a silence*]

PAUL: I'm not sure what my attitude to all this is other than a deep sense of shock, but I am your son, and I am a Christian, and if there's anything I can do I'll try and do it.

SUSY: Paul, don't be so bloody pious. He groped me, I whacked him, end of story.

BRIAN: It was unforgivable.

SUSY: Dad, just shut up! Just shut up!

KATY: Susy.

SUSY: [*agitated*] I just don't know how to handle this, OK? I don't know what we're supposed to do! Not the sex thing. The illness, the money!

PAUL: Do what you usually do. Run!

BRIAN: Just do nothing. I mean it.

* * *

The conference room. SUSY, KATY *and* MARION *are there.* GARY *enters.*

MARION: Where's Vince?

GARY: Vince isn't the owner of the business any more. I am.

Lies Lies Lies Lies Lies Lies Lies Lies Lies Lies

SUSY: You are?
GARY: As good as. The documents have been signed. A management buyout, funded by two merchant banks.
SUSY: So what's happened to Vince? Dumped?
GARY: Yeah, dumped. It happens all the time. Shall we start?
KATY: So if you're the owner I guess the firm pays the entire settlement?
GARY: There's going to be no settlement. And if this goes any longer than today, I'll be taking out a defamation action against your sister.
MARION: All the discussions in here are privileged. You can't sue.
GARY: You better tell my lawyer that. He thinks I can.
SUSY: I'll take it to the tribunal.
GARY: You haven't got a shred of evidence and no one's going to believe a word you say. Honey, your arse is grass and I'm the lawnmower.
SUSY: What about the publicity?
GARY: I'm not worried about it and neither is my wife and family. You're the one who's going to make a fool of yourself.
SUSY: You're really going to put me in my place, eh Gary?
GARY: A man isn't worth anything if he lets himself cave in to a tissue of lies.
SUSY: *Real* men don't take shit from women do they, Gary? I guess we go to tribunal.
GARY: Good. I've hired an investigator to do a check on your lifestyle and I think you're going to find it very hard toargue in court that a few mild remarks over the phone would cause you much distress.
KATY: You hired an investigator?
GARY: Absolutely. I regard this as an extortion attempt and I've reacted accordingly. In the three years before you started work with us you lived with five men and had sex with at least five others. Hardly a coy little innocent are you?

SUSY: OK, Gary. I gave you a chance. I think it's time to tell the real story.
GARY: We know the real story. A few phone calls.
SUSY: OK, Gary, let's do it. [*To* MARION] The real story is that I did egg him on at the start.
GARY: First truthful thing I've heard you say.
SUSY: Believe it or not I even found him quite attractive.
GARY: Finally she admits it. *gives himself*
SUSY: He took me out for lunch, and pretty soon it became physical.
GARY: That's bullshit!
SUSY: Lunchtime sex. I'd walk round the corner, he'd pick me up in his car. Five minute drive to my place –
GARY: Bullshit!
SUSY: And be well gone before my sister got home at three. It was pretty wild for a while –
GARY: Bullshit!
MARION: Gary, could we just hear this version. You'll get your say shortly.
GARY: It's all lies!
MARION: [*angrily*] Just shut up!
SUSY: But pretty soon, I had one of my 'where is my life going?' flashes. And the answer, seemed to be 'not where I want it to go'. Why am I sleeping with a guy I don't even like, who's married with kids, who makes a living by lying to clients who trust him, and who makes love as if it's some kind of – violent punishment.
GARY: I never went near you, you bitch!
SUSY: When I told Gary that the party was over, he didn't take it at all well. Gary's sense of himself requires that he discards women, they don't discard him. The phone calls started and they were vile, but I was determined to hang on to my job for at least a year.
GARY: You're surely not *believing* any of this?!
MARION: [*tersely*] Gary. We know you've got a different version. Can we please hear this first!

SUSY: I've been called all kinds of things. I'm not exactly a delicate flower, but some of the things he said over the phone really shook me. I suppose I should've left, but I said no, bugger it. OK, I started it, but I very quickly realised my mistake and I think I had a right to finish it without getting this.

GARY: I'm sorry, but I'm not listening to this.

MARION: You're going to have to listen to it in court Gary. I'd advise you to get used to it.

GARY: You've been on her side all the way. All the bloody way!

MARION: [*losing her temper*] With someone like you around it's very hard not to be!

GARY: You're on her side. You're admitting it!

KATY: [*loudly*] Gary, shut up!

SUSY: Sure, I know men get angry when they're rejected. That's normal, but what Gary started to do wasn't normal. He didn't just want to punish me, he seemed to want to annihilate me.

GARY: You expect me to just sit here quietly and listen to this?

KATY: If you don't let her finish I'll ram your bloody Mazda!

SUSY: This isn't easy for me, Gary. You've got a problem, let's address it.

GARY: Problem? You've got the problem!

MARION: What was he saying to you?

SUSY: Humiliation fantasies. Full of aggression and contempt. Trying to degrade me.

KATY: You're sick, Gary. Really sick.

GARY: [*to* SUSY] This is full on libel. You're gone! Sure, I'll listen. I'll listen to every word. I'm noting it down.

SUSY: I knew by now I was dealing with someone who had an immense hostility for women he could barely control.

GARY: [*to* MARION] Do you believe this!

MARION: Look at the way you're behaving now! You don't think you're hostile?

ACT TWO

GARY: No! I'm legitimately angry and if you can't tell the difference between legitimate anger and hostility you shouldn't be doing this job! [*To* SUSY] Go on. More lies. Just remember I'm noting them down.

SUSY: I knew I couldn't stay at the job much longer unless I organised a cease-fire. Stupidly, I thought that the night we worked back, with just the two of us there, I could maybe talk him through it. It turned out to be the worst night of my life.

[SUSY *starts to get very upset.* KATY *moves towards her to comfort her.*]

GARY: We're going to get tears as well now? Academy awards eat your heart out.

SUSY: [*angrily*] Gary face it. You're a sick human being. Is that the way you want to be all your life! As soon as everyone was gone he shut the door and he went right off his face. He screamed that his wife treated him like shit, and that *I'd* treated him like shit and if I wanted to keep my job here I was going to get down on my knees, crawl to him across the carpet, and give him oral sex. I went to the door, but he'd locked it. I told him I'd scream, he said 'Scream away, no one will hear –'

GARY: [*angrily*] You're going to spend the rest of your life paying for this! I hope you've got a good lawyer!

SUSY: He ranted on at me -

MARION: About what?

[SUSY *begins to cry quietly and shakes her head as if she cannot bear to go on.* KATY *hugs her.*]

SUSY: About women being two-faced bitches who demanded equality then turned round and used the same old 'pussy power' they'd been using since Cleopatra's time. And how when his wife found out he'd had an affair she woke up his daughters and told them about their father, the adulterer. And how she gets more pleasure out of her vibrator than him. And how he hated her so much that the

only thing that made him feel good was that he'd cheated on her four times since.
GARY: [*ashen*] Don't try this on. Stephanie's right behind me.
SUSY: I finally thought, 'This guy is crazy. I've got to get out of here. Anything is better than this'. So I got down on my knees, crawled towards him, closed my eyes because I couldn't stand the sight of him, and suddenly found myself choking on a fifty dollar note.
GARY: You've got to be joking. I'd waste fifty dollars on you!?
SUSY: So yes. I wasn't telling the total truth. I was the one who started it, but I think I still have the right to finish it without getting that.

[*There is a silence.* MARION *and* KATY *are shocked*]

MARION: Would you be prepared to tell that version to the tribunal?
SUSY: Yes.
GARY: You don't believe this?

[MARION *looks at* SUSY, *sobbing quietly in her sister's arms.*]

MARION: Am I supposed to believe that's an act?
GARY: Of course it's an act.
MARION: I find it very convincing, and I think a jury will too.
KATY: You're sick, Gary. Do yourself a favour and go and see a shrink.
GARY: [*enraged*] I'm out of here! [*To all of them*] You're all the same!

[*He storms out.*]

SUSY: So that's the truth. I *did* start it so maybe forty thousand *is* too much to claim.
MARION: Maybe, but he did treat you appallingly, and I've got a feeling he'll pay.
SUSY: You think?
MARION: The last thing he'd want to hear is that story in court.

ACT TWO

SUSY: I'm sorry I lied. I guess I couldn't face admitting that I fell for that macho stuff at the start.
MARION: Too many of us do. At the start.

* * *

Outside the building.

KATY: Was that all true?
SUSY: [*indignantly*] Yes! What do you think? I lie all the time!
KATY: It was true? All of it?
SUSY: Yes!
　　　[KATY *looks at her.* SUSY *shrugs.*]
　　All except the fifty dollars.
　　　[KATY *looks at her.*]
KATY: Susy, you are truly frightening.
SUSY: The other stuff was absolutely true. He's crazy. Whenever he said his wife's name I thought he was going to kill me.
KATY: Lunchtime sex with Gary. Was that true?
SUSY: [*nodding*] Yes.
KATY: Even if I was straight I still couldn't imagine it.
SUSY: He's got energy.
KATY: So has an electric toaster but you don't have sex with it.
SUSY: Marion thinks we'll get the money.
KATY: And it's for Dad.
SUSY: No way Katy. That money is for us. We deserve a chance!
KATY: How will you feel if he dies?
SUSY: If he was Bob Geldorf or someone yeah, but he's basically a sleaze!
KATY: Susy, you're giving him the money.
SUSY: We're taking from one sleaze to help another.
KATY: The second sleaze is your father.

SUSY: [*darkly*] By Christ, he better be grateful!

* * *

BRIAN's *back garden.* BRIAN *is looking healthier, more cheerful. He sits there beaming.* PAUL *is there looking morose.* KATY *looking calm and* SUSY *pacing up and down looking irritated.*

BRIAN: When the surgeons opened me up they said they knew immediately I wouldn't have lasted the distance. So the fact that I'm sitting here today owes everything to you, Susy.
SUSY: Now that we've paid the money, what are we going to get? How do you intend to spend your next ten years?
BRIAN: You'd like value for money?
SUSY: Actually I would. What do you intend to do with your life, because I tell you what, mine's looking pretty grim.
BRIAN: Katy said you got a new job.
SUSY: Wordprocessing in John Howard's office. There's a job with a future. What about you?
BRIAN: I've phoned a very old friend and proposed.
KATY: Proposed what? Marriage?
BRIAN: Marriage. I want a real, loving, full relationship.
KATY: Who?
BRIAN: Gwen Mountjoy.
SUSY: Gwen Mountjoy? Thirty thousand dollars to see Gwen Mountjoy stumble down the aisle?
BRIAN: She's cut back on her drinking.
SUSY: Like you have? You'll certainly get a full relationship with Gwen.
BRIAN: [*angrily*] I appreciate what you've done for me, Susy and I will try and live the last years of my life decently. What more can I say?
SUSY: You can say thank you to Katy. She made me hand the money over.

ACT TWO 71

BRIAN: I'm sure she didn't.
SUSY: She did. Don't fool yourself. If it had've been up to me we would have been down at alcoholics anonymous now scattering your ashes.
PAUL: I would have helped, Dad. If there was any *way* I could have raised the money I would have helped.
BRIAN: I know son. I know.
PAUL: I feel so badly that I didn't contribute.
BRIAN: You're in debt.
PAUL: I shouldn't be. I should've been well in the black by now.
BRIAN: It's not your fault. Business was never going to be your forte. You were always the sort of kid who could never quite get his act together.
PAUL: [*hurt*] I got my act together in one way, at least.
BRIAN: I wasn't trying to be rude, Paul. You're a great kid. I love you just as much as your sisters.
PAUL: A lot of sons would've been so appalled at what they heard that they'd never speak to you again.
KATY: Paul, it's not the day to be moralistic.
PAUL: [*moralistically*] I'm not being moralistic. I coped with it. I'm here. I forgave. But it's obvious now why I didn't get any gold American Express cards.
BRIAN: Paul, it was just one or two unfortunate incidents –
SUSY: One or two? Katy lost count!
KATY: Susy!
BRIAN: That's a lie!
SUSY: Why don't you apologise to her some time, Dad! She's the reason you're alive today!
BRIAN: I'm sorry! OK. I'm sorry. A father who's drunk a bit too much gives his daughters a playful tweak! Big deal!
SUSY: More than a tweak!
BRIAN: A tweak. Jesus!
PAUL: Please don't say Jesus.
BRIAN: If that's all it takes to ruin your lives then pity help you!

KATY: You've got no idea, have you? To you it was just a funny little game you played and why the hell are we making such a fuss?
BRIAN: I said I'm sorry. What more do you want?
SUSY: We want you to *mean* it!
BRIAN: One day you bloody feminists are going to realise that men *aren't* like women. We have a sex drive that's demanding and insistent!
SUSY: So men can rape women, fathers molest daughters – and it's never their fault? They just have these tacky little testicular tadpoles that force them to behave like arseholes. Great argument, Dad!
KATY: We *all* have a sex drive, Dad! Most of us are mature enough to control it!
BRIAN: Control yourself, control yourself – you're just like your mother!
KATY: Don't bring her into this!
BRIAN: Your mother was a wonderful, wonderful, wonderful – I'll give you as many wonderfuls as you like – woman, but she was as frigid as a Hobart summer!
KATY: Don't you *dare* blame your behaviour on Mum!
SUSY: What are you saying, Dad? Because Mum wasn't as sex obsessed as you were it was OK to touch *us* up?
BRIAN: A few playful tweaks!
PAUL: [*angrily*] Dad, don't keep minimising it! OK I know you never listen to anything I ever say – I know I'm the family joke, but at least I know enough to realise that what you did was not normal, not civilised and not bloody acceptable!

[BRIAN *is jolted by his son's fiery outburst.*]

KATY: I just want you to know something, Dad. I had fantasies for years that the best thing I could do for Mum was to kill you!

[*Pause*]

I still dream about it.

[BRIAN *looks at* KATY, *then back at* PAUL.]

SUSY: Dad, we trusted you. You were like God. Charming, funny, loving – trust you with our lives – then suddenly we turn thirteen and we're just two tits on legs. Have you any *idea* how that feels? Have you?
KATY: We don't *want* to hate you, Dad!
   [BRIAN *stares at them, the message slowly sinking in.*]
I remember once when I was about ten or eleven I was at a party. Mum had dressed me up to look as pretty as possible. When you arrived you heard some boys teasing me and saw me crying my eyes out, so you walked up to the ringleader and said, 'If I had ears that stuck out like jug handles, a chin that didn't exist and a body odour that could kill at ten paces, I'd think twice before I ridiculed anyone else'. Then spent the next two hours reassuring me. I've never felt more grateful to anyone in my life.
SUSY: We don't *want* to hate you, Dad.
KATY: We used to love you so much, and we miss that.
   [*A long pause*]
BRIAN: I'm sorry. Admitting I'm wrong has never come easily to me, but if what I did made you feel like that then I'm appalled I never realised it. I'm truly sorry.
   [*Another pause.* KATY *and* SUSY *look at each other.*]
Susy and Katy, thank you. I'm incredibly grateful for what you've done for me. Thank you. And Paul, thank you too –
   [*Pause*]
You're all great kids despite me, so here's to – my family.
   [BRIAN *raises his glass to them. The two sisters look at each other.*]
KATY: Well, I guess any institution that can incorporate sociopaths, child molesters, homosexuals and Christians who still manage to speak to one another, must have something going for it.
   [*They drink.* BRIAN *raises his glass again.*]
BRIAN: And to harmony between the sexes.
KATY: Dad, let's not get carried away.

SUSY: Let's just drink to a truce.
 [*They raise their glasses and drink.*]

THE END